BASICS
FILM

the language of film

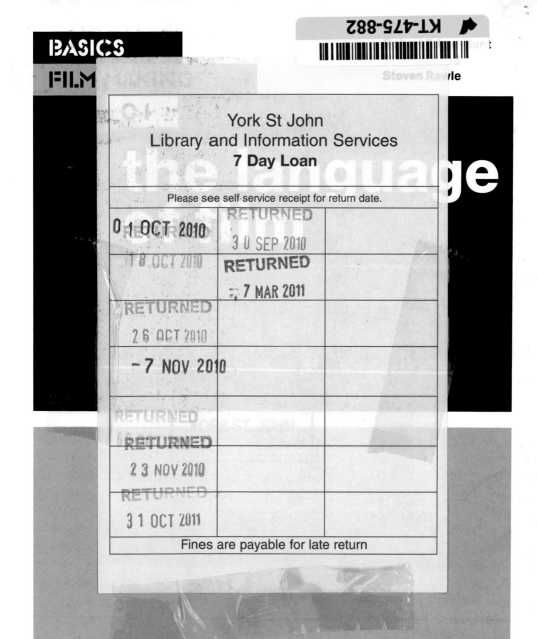

ethical:
aware-
ness/
reflect-
ion/
debate

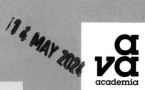

ava
academia

An AVA Book

Published by AVA Publishing SA
Rue des Fontenailles 16
Case Postale
1000 Lausanne 6
Switzerland
Tel: +41 786 005 109
Email: enquiries@avabooks.ch

Distributed by Thames & Hudson
(ex-North America)
181a High Holborn
London WC1V 7QX
United Kingdom
Tel: +44 20 7845 5000
Fax: +44 20 7845 5055
Email: sales@thameshudson.co.uk
www.thamesandhudson.com

Distributed in the USA & Canada by:
Ingram Publisher Services Inc.
1 Ingram Blvd.
La Vergne TN 37086
USA
Tel: +1 866 400 5351
Fax: +1 800 838 1149
E-mail: customer.service@
ingrampublisherservices.com

English Language Support Office
AVA Publishing (UK) Ltd.
Tel: +44 1903 204 455
Email: enquiries@avabooks.ch

ISBN 978-2-940411-27-6

10 9 8 7 6 5 4 3 2 1

Design by Darren Lever

Production by AVA Book Production Pte. Ltd.,
Singapore
Tel: +65 6334 8173
Fax: +65 6259 9830
Email: production@avabooks.com.sg

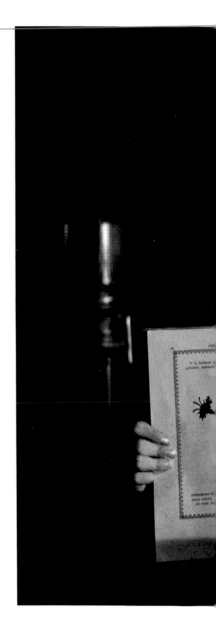

Pan's Labyrinth
(dir: Guillermo del Toro 2006)

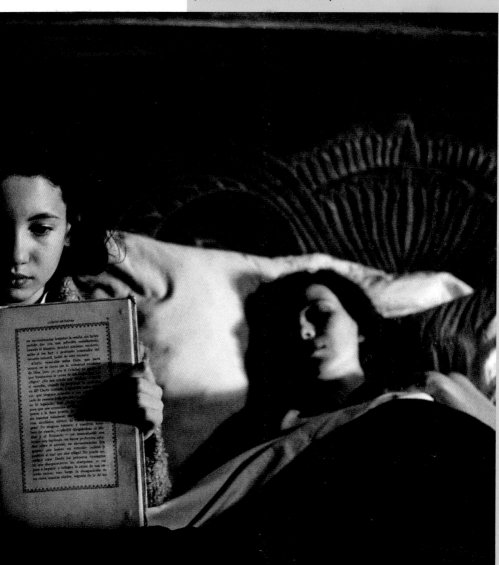

Pan's Labyrinth combines fantasy with social commentary and political debate. Part of the power of cinema is to engage us in spectacle whilst intellectually challenging us. This is part of the language of film and is one of the reasons why this language is so specific to cinema.

Table of contents

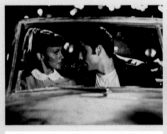

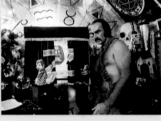

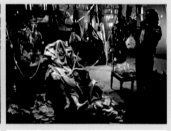

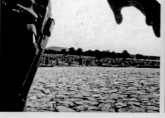

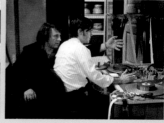

Table of contents

How to get the most out of this book

The Language of Film is constructed in six chapters that cover different but related areas. The chapters can be read out of sequence, but like any good narrative it is better to start at the beginning and work through. In this way, you will build your knowledge and then be able to branch into the specific areas that interest you. The chapters all contain exercises, tips, further reading and case studies.

Throughout the book we will encourage you to watch as many films as you can; get through as many genres, movements, historical periods, countries and cultures as possible. You don't have to be a film historian or a cultural theorist to understand the language of film, but knowledge of the diversity of work available is invaluable. Start off with examples that are familiar, that are useful and that will aid you in your journey as a practitioner, as a theorist or hopefully as both.

A running glossary explains key terms clearly and precisely

Captions illustrate stills from a range of classic and student films

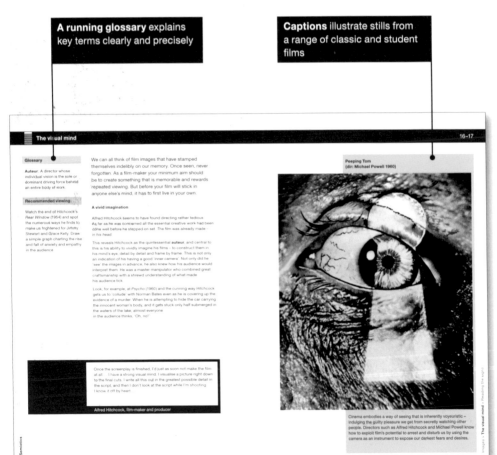

Glossary

Auteur: A director whose individual vision is the sole or dominant driving force behind an entire body of work.

Recommended viewing

Watch the end of Hitchcock's *Rear Window* (1954) and spot the numerous ways he finds to make us frightened for Jimmy Stewart and Grace Kelly. Draw a simple graph charting the rise and fall of anxiety and empathy in the audience.

We can all think of film images that have stamped themselves indelibly on our memory. Once seen, never forgotten. As a film-maker your minimum aim should be to create something that is memorable and rewards repeated viewing. But before your film will stick in anyone else's mind, it has to first live in your own.

A vivid imagination

Alfred Hitchcock seems to have found directing rather tedious. As far as he was concerned all the essential creative work had been done well before he stepped on set. The film was already made – in his head.

This reveals Hitchcock as the quintessential *auteur*, and central to this is his ability to vividly imagine his films – to construct them in his mind's eye, detail by detail and frame by frame. This is not only an indication of his having a good 'inner camera'. Not only did he 'see' the images in advance, he also knew how his audience would interpret them. He was a master manipulator who combined great craftsmanship with a shrewd understanding of what made his audience tick.

Look, for example, at *Psycho* (1960) and the cunning way Hitchcock gets us to 'collude' with Norman Bates even as he is covering up the evidence of a murder. When he is attempting to hide the car carrying the innocent woman's body, and it gets stuck only half submerged in the waters of the lake, almost everyone in the audience thinks, 'Oh, no!'

> Once the screenplay is finished, I'd just as soon not make the film at all ... I have a strong visual mind. I visualise a picture right down to the final cuts. I write all this out in the greatest possible detail in the script, and then I don't look at the script while I'm shooting. I know it off by heart.

Alfred Hitchcock, film-maker and producer

Peeping Tom
(dir: Michael Powell 1960)

Cinema embodies a way of seeing that is inherently voyeuristic – indulging the guilty pleasure we get from secretly watching other people. Directors such as Alfred Hitchcock and Michael Powell know how to exploit film's potential to arrest and disturb us by using the camera as an instrument to expose our darkest fears and desires.

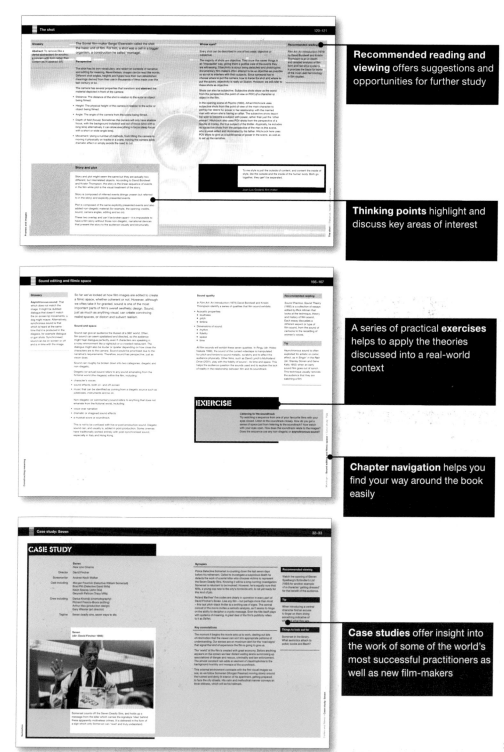

Recommended reading and viewing offers suggestions and opportunities for further study

Thinking points highlight and discuss key areas of interest

A series of practical **exercises** helps to apply the theories discussed into a real-world context

Chapter navigation helps you find your way around the book easily

Case studies offer insight into the work of some of the world's most successful practitioners as well as new film-makers

How to get the most out of this book

As the title of this book suggests, film has a distinctive language all of its own.

When we are watching a movie in the cinema or at home we seldom have any difficulty understanding this language. Even though most films are a mosaic of fractured images and fragmented narratives, we have little problem piecing them together into something complete, pleasing and meaningful (so much so that we seldom experience them as fractured or fragmented in the first place). We are capable of following the most labyrinthine plots, feeling genuine emotion for the most improbable characters, and believing that their worlds continue to exist even after the film has ended. We don't know how we do it (or that we are *doing* anything at all) but we are.

We never had to learn 'film'. We are like people who had no need to learn the grammar of their 'mother tongue' because it has come so naturally to them, merely by being exposed to it. However, becoming a film-maker involves being deliberately mindful of the structures and conventions that allow film to communicate so effectively to a global audience. An effective film-maker needs to know how this language works, how the screen communicates to people, how meaning is gradually built up of tiny elements, and how to control an audience's thoughts and feeling.

It isn't enough to be able to 'read' the screen, you need to be able to 'write' on it. The *implicit* knowledge we have as spectators has to be converted into the *explicit* knowledge of the practitioner who can *make* these things happen *for someone else* – who can create narrative complexity, stimulate feelings towards fictional characters, and generally suspend the disbelief of an entire movie theatre. In other words, film-makers need to learn how to create the experiences that audiences crave – and harness the power of illusion that makes film such a uniquely popular medium.

This book attempts to help you to make the transition from consumer to practitioner – from someone who just responds to the language of film, to someone who actively *uses* it.

Film is one of three universal languages, the other two: mathematics and music.

Frank Capra, director

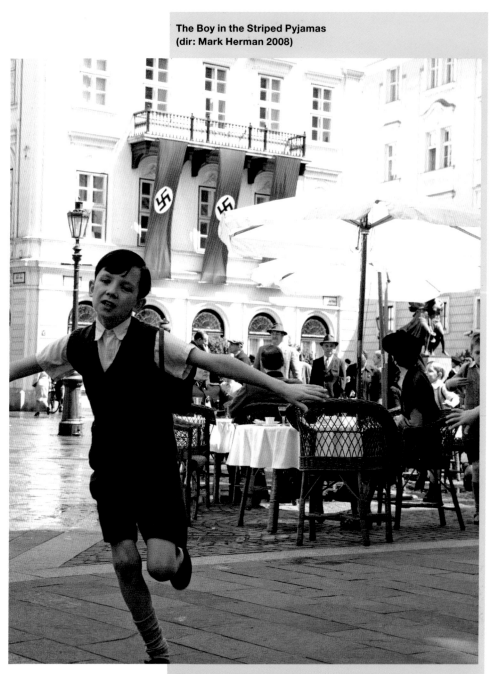

The Boy in the Striped Pyjamas
(dir: Mark Herman 2008)

The Boy in the Striped Pyjamas takes the audience on an emotional journey into history and imagination. The flickering lights (which all film is made from) convey a story of great power in personalising the horrors of the Holocaust.

Introduction

Starting again

Ironically, the ease with which we consume film presents us with a problem. The very immediacy of film, its spectacle, and the directness of its impact on us, make it difficult to unpick and examine. We have to 'unlearn' a lot of what we think we know, and start again. For this reason we will go back to the basic first principles from which all films grow.

Our familiarity with the form actually makes it more difficult to think about film constructively. This is what is most valuable about film theory, and why we shall be referring to some key theoretical thinkers – they have the happy knack of making us look again at what we take for granted.

One such film theorist, Christian Metz, famously said that: 'Film is hard to explain, because it is so easy to understand.' Here Metz is making the crucial distinction between knowing what a thing means and knowing how it comes to have that meaning, between 'tacit' knowing and the sort of knowledge that can be readily articulated to others. Film-makers – be they directors, cinematographers, designers or actors – need to be able to talk to one another about what they are doing, about the 'meaning' they are trying to create. Only then can they really be said to be working collaboratively in this most collaborative of art forms.

Film languages

Film language is actually made up of many different languages all subsumed into one medium. Film can co-opt into itself all the other arts – photography, painting, theatre, music, architecture, dance and of course, the spoken word. Everything can find its way into a movie – large or small, natural or fantastic, beautiful or grotesque.

Not that film is without limitations. There are things that cinema struggles to do. The very fact that it is a predominantly visual medium makes invisible things (the stuff of the mind and the heart) impossible to convey except indirectly. Unlike a novel, a film cannot take us into the unconscious thoughts or secret longings of a character. We can only know of these things indirectly – by interpreting what we see of their external behaviour.

This is a limitation indeed, but the same one we experience in real life!

Chapter by chapter

Chapter 1: Semiotics

Film, like any 'language', is composed of signs. Film semiotics is the study of how these visual and auditory units function to construct the meaning we attribute to cinematic texts. Film-makers and audiences share an understanding of the sign systems (the codes and conventions) that allow film to communicate meanings beyond what is seen or heard. Chapter 1 seeks to investigate and outline these codes and conventions.

Chapter 2: Narrative

The consideration of narrative is the consideration of how an audience derives meaning from a film – it is about comprehension. In Chapter 2, we'll see how films are limited by time, and by their own language, and thus why their structure has to be very precise. Generally, the more successful a film is the more hidden its structure will be. It is your job to uncover that structure.

Chapter 3: Intertextuality

Texts are not produced or consumed in a vacuum, but in the context of other textual activity. Films relate to each other. Textual production occurs against a dense background of expectations, established by tradition and perpetuated by generic conventions. Textual 'meaning' arises as the result of a process of recognition, comparison and contrast to which all texts are subject. In Chapter 3, this 'intertextuality' is examined to suggest some of the various ways film begets film begets film.

Chapter 4: Ideology

Chapter 4 examines the question of what films mean. The interpretations people give to films are many and varied but what is without doubt is that film always carries a message or messages. This chapter seeks to determine that all film and all aspects of film are ideological and the choices an audience has as to the meaning are actually very limited. They are limited by context, by expectation and by the maker(s) of the film.

Chapter 5: Frames and images

In Chapter 5 we'll look at how the 'seen' aspects of cinema relate to the ways in which the camera gives us a perspective on what we see and how we comprehend the many possible uses of the image. The various visual uses of the film image will be examined through the vocabulary of the moving image and a series of case studies to show how the film camera shapes and distorts our perspective of cinematic objects and spaces.

Chapter 6: Constructing meaning

In addition to the visual aesthetics of the camera, cinema has a substantial array of 'unseen' techniques relating to the ways in which images are joined together through editing and sound. Space, time, narrative and style are all constructed by the use of editing techniques to manipulate the individual images into a coherent (or deliberately incoherent) whole. In Chapter 6, we'll consider these 'invisible' effects to see how editing adds another dimension to the visual image.

The chapters are interspersed with case studies, exercises, and a selection of recommended viewing and recommended reading suggestions.

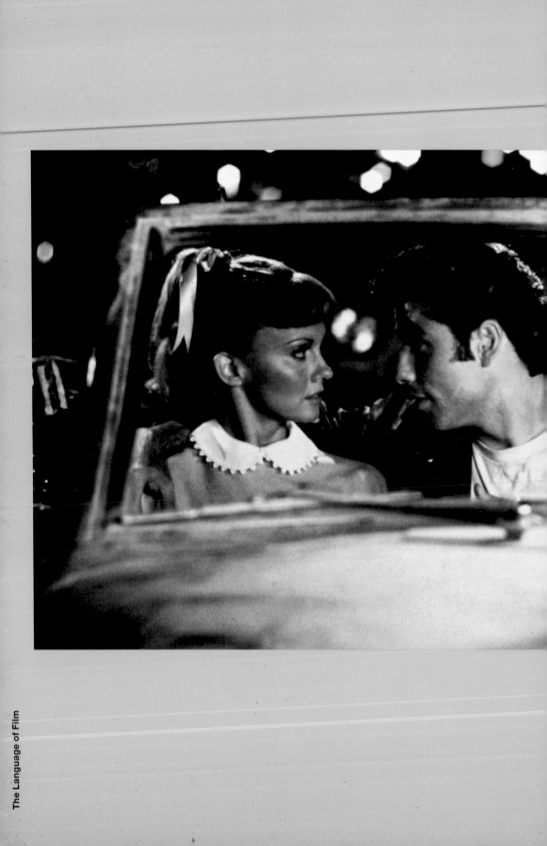

SEMIOTICS

Grease
(dir: Randal Kleiser 1978)

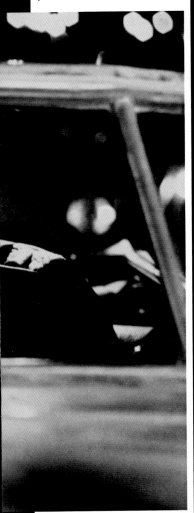

Every picture tells a story. It's remarkable what can be read from a single image. Even if we haven't seen the complete film we already 'know' a great deal about Danny and Sandy from the information contained in this one frame. Semiotics investigates how this is possible.

Basically, film-making is telling a story in pictures.

This sounds pretty straightforward. Simply let the camera roll, record the actors speaking their lines, and your film will be 'in the can' in no time. Capture enough footage and you can always pull it into the desired shape later on. Right?

Wrong! Holidaymakers can afford to do this, proper *film-makers* can't. Leaving the story to play itself out in front of a camera is wasteful of both time and money, and will almost always result in something as awkward, slow, drab and stagey as the average wedding video. The camera is not responsible for the pictures on the screen – *you are*.

Real movie-making begins with carefully choosing the precise images you *need* for the particular story you want to *tell*. This selection process is done in the best equipped editing room in the world – your imagination.

This leads inevitably to the study of semiotics; this is essentially the study of 'signs', it is the analysis of communication and can be applied to any form of communication. Film has its own language and therefore there is a branch of semiotics which concerns itself with film.

Film-makers have the biggest canvas and the fullest paintbox imaginable. With it they can fashion images that speak to virtually anyone who sees them.

Visual culture

One look at the still from *Grease* on page 12, and we feel we understand exactly what is going on. This is because everything has been arranged to ensure we do.

The shot is framed to emphasise the way Danny (John Travolta) is 'making advances' toward Sandy (Olivia Newton-John) – invading her space. It is obviously *his* car – and a *red* one at that. The white T-shirt and black leather jacket, regulation wear for a young rock 'n' roller, conform to the stereotype of disaffected youth created by actors such as Marlon Brando. His thick glossy jet-black quiff and sideburns are the signatures of his manhood, dangerous and wild. This is who he is, or rather who we are meant to think he is. Sandy is also instantly recognisable. Her cardigan, high-buttoned blouse and lace collar put her at the opposite end of conformity and respectability. The costume makes her a 'good girl' in contrast to his 'bad boy'. Her hairstyle is as virginal as his *isn't*. The film goes on to have fun with these notions. Danny isn't really so 'bad' but has to keep up the pretence in front of his friends. The all-singing, all-dancing finale has them swap personas – sacrificing their 'reputation' to prove their true feelings for each other. So Danny turns up at the 'School's Out' celebrations dressed like a college kid, while Sandy is transformed into a leather-clad vamp complete with cascading curls, red lipstick and chewing gum. She even stubs out a cigarette in *dangerously* high heels. For the transformation to work, the images must be clear and precise, and we must be able to 'read' them.

In fact, we seem to pick up these signals quite effortlessly. This is because we belong to a visual culture adept at the transmission and reception of visual information. Film-makers in particular need to be experts in this process.

Seeing comes before words.

John Berger, art critic, novelist, painter

Semiotics

Precision

Film images are *never* vague. They are stubbornly 'concrete'. You may casually envisage a scene in terms of *a* man, *a* car, and *a* landscape. However, the camera will slavishly record *this* man, in *this* car, on *this* landscape – in all their specificity. The image will immediately convey a huge number of impressions (such as period and location) and suggest a host of ideas (such as romantic journeys, the open road or the vastness of nature).

Are these the thoughts you want the audience to have? If you show Danny in his car the audience will think of 1950s America, 'free spirit' and 'trouble ahead'. Successful film-making depends on having a firm command of your material – exercising maximum control over what the viewers see and hear.

It is often the little things that count the most: for example, in a wedding scene it might be the gleam in the bride's eye or the rather proud way she holds her head; the way the groom fiddles with his tie or fires a glance at another woman in the congregation; the stilted walk of the bride's father and the tear on her mother's cheek; the fidgeting children at the back and the panicky expression on the best man's face as he checks his pockets for the ring.

All these are wedding-scene **clichés**, but if they are chosen and arranged with sufficient care, then the tension for the audience in the cinema is as great as it would be for the guests in the church. The excitement and trepidation pours from the screen into the auditorium.

With all the above in place you can be sure your audience will jump when the bride calmly lifts her veil, slowly withdraws a knife from beneath her bouquet and stabs the bridegroom straight through the heart. Now there's a wedding scene! And what of the final image: the flower in his button-hole, slowly turning from white to red? Not subtle, but indelible – *and worth a thousand words.*

Glossary

Clichés: Overused, stale and out-worn expressions, mostly to be avoided. But they are overused for a reason – they tend to *work*, especially when given a slight 'tweak'.

Recommended reading

Roland Barthes' *Mythologies* is a collection of articles written between 1954 and 1956 for the left-wing French magazine *Les lettres nouvelles*. The articles show how even seemingly trivial aspects of everyday life can be filled with meaning and are wonderfully playful about 'the little things'– including the meaning of Marlon Brando's hairstyle in the film *Julius Caesar* (dir: Joseph L. Mankiewicz 1953).

Images > The visual mind

The visual mind

Glossary

Auteur: A director whose individual vision is the sole or dominant driving force behind an entire body of work.

Recommended viewing

Watch the end of Hitchcock's *Rear Window* (1954) and spot the numerous ways he finds to make us frightened for Jimmy Stewart and Grace Kelly. Draw a simple graph charting the rise and fall of anxiety and empathy in the audience.

We can all think of film images that have stamped themselves indelibly on our memory. Once seen, never forgotten. As a film-maker your minimum aim should be to create something that is memorable and rewards repeated viewing. But before your film will stick in anyone else's mind, it has to first live in your own.

A vivid imagination

Alfred Hitchcock seems to have found directing rather tedious. As far as he was concerned all the essential creative work had been done well before he stepped on set. The film was already made – *in his head*.

This reveals Hitchcock as the quintessential **auteur**, and central to this is his ability to vividly imagine his films – to construct them in his mind's eye, detail by detail and frame by frame. This is not only an indication of his having a good 'inner camera'. Not only did he 'see' the images in advance, he also knew how his audience would interpret them. He was a master manipulator who combined great craftsmanship with a shrewd understanding of what made his audience tick.

Look, for example, at *Psycho* (1960) and the cunning way Hitchcock gets us to 'collude' with Norman Bates even as he is covering up the evidence of a murder. When he is attempting to hide the car carrying the innocent woman's body, and it gets stuck only half submerged in the waters of the lake, almost everyone in the audience thinks, 'Oh, no!'

Once the screenplay is finished, I'd just as soon not make the film at all…. I have a strong visual mind. I visualise a picture right down to the final cuts. I write all this out in the greatest possible detail in the script, and then I don't look at the script while I'm shooting. I know it off by heart….

Alfred Hitchcock, film-maker and producer

**Peeping Tom
(dir: Michael Powell 1960)**

Cinema embodies a way of seeing that is inherently voyeuristic –
indulging the guilty pleasure we get from secretly watching other
people. Directors such as Alfred Hitchcock and Michael Powell know
how to exploit film's potential to arrest and disturb us by using the
camera as an instrument to expose our darkest fears and desires.

Glossary

Semiotics: The study of signs. It has its origins in the work of Ferdinand de Saussure, a Swiss linguist who was the first to identify some of the basic principles that apply to any sign-based system.

Sign: An object, quality or event whose presence or occurrence indicates the probable presence or occurrence of something else.

A movie is a highly complex act of communication, and no act of communication is effective unless it takes into account how the recipient will receive it. If a film is to have the desired effect, the film-maker needs to know exactly how the screen communicates. They need to know how the images produced will be understood by the audience and work upon their imaginations moment by moment. This is where **semiotics** is useful.

Units of meaning

When we talk about movies we typically refer to characters, action and dialogue. In fact each of these elements is made up of much smaller units. Characters, for instance, are built from tiny fragments of information (such as physical features, bodily gestures and spoken words) each selected and juxtaposed to create the illusion of a real-life three-dimensional human being.

Film theorists refer to a detail of this sort as a **sign**. Film semiotics, the study of cinematic signs, breaks film down into its constituent parts to identify the atomic building blocks from which the complexity of narrative is constructed. Signs are the most fundamental units of meaning – the atoms from which films are formed.

A sign is anything we can see or hear or feel that refers to something we can't – usually something absent or abstract. For example, the sign we commonly see by the roadside illustrating a man digging is there to warn us of roadworks or potential hazards not yet visible.

In the specific context of cinema a 'sign' is anything, large or small, which we find ourselves responding to. Put another way, something *becomes* a sign when we single it out for special attention. For instance, we may take no real notice of anything outside the car as we watch the family having a violent argument, but once we hear the sound of a pneumatic drill and spot the workmen with their shovels these become 'danger signs'.

Visual abbreviation

Imagine a Western. The ringing of a church bell is an ominous sign. A crowd gathered around a body lying in the middle of Main Street is a sign that there has been a gunfight. The badge on his shirt indicates that he was the sheriff – it's a sign of his status. The sight of another man removing it and pinning it on himself is yet another sign, either that the sheriff's deputy is taking over the job or that a gunman is taking control of the town.

Anything the eye or ear picks up on, whatever we single out for attention and draw a specific meaning from, is functioning as a sign. It stands for something that contributes to our overall understanding. The sheriff's grey beard may be a sign that he was too old for the job. The gun still in his holster is a sign he was hopelessly outclassed, taken by surprise or shot in the back. Amid this field of *implicit* signs is a single *explicit* one – a crumpled poster carrying the gunman's picture and the word 'wanted'.

A sign is not always so clear-cut. A scar on the deputy's face might indicate that he too is a victim of violence. On the gunman it would signal that he habitually *deals* in violence – he is a villain. Context determines the exact meaning we derive from a sign, and this context is made up of other signs. A smile on the gunman's lips would tell us how to read the scar on his cheek.

Film is the art of visual abbreviation. Film-makers use smiles and scars, badges and beards, to tell the audience more than they can be explicitly shown or told. The audience sees meaning in them because it is a movie – and they have been deliberately placed there for a reason. A movie is a matrix of interrelated signs erected by the film-maker to guide the audience on their journey.

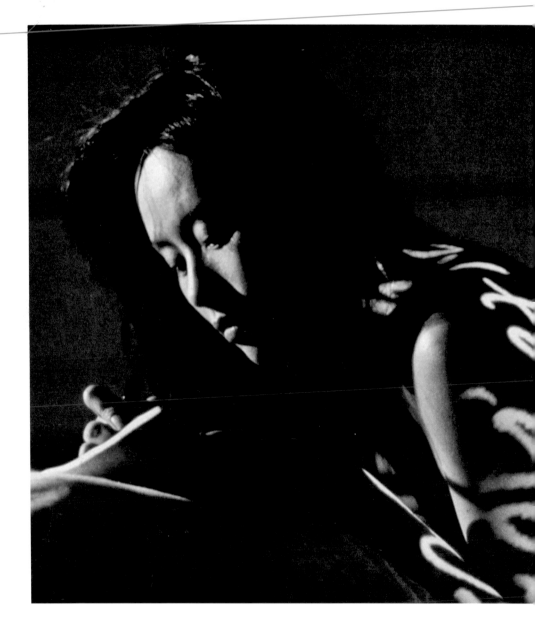

The Pillow Book
(dir: Peter Greenaway 1996)

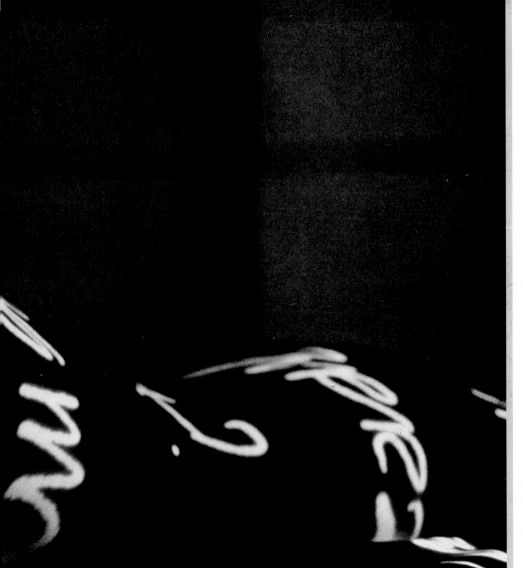

It has been said that film-making is 'painting with light'. Well, here the words projected onto a woman's body create an unusual connection between the subject and the viewer. She is reading signs and so are we. Greenaway knows that overlaying images not only creates aesthetic depth, but intellectual complexity.

A compound of signs

The still from *The Pillow Book* on pages 20–21 is an unusually intricate image. In a sense, the reclining figure is itself a compound of signs from which we gather an impression of luxuriant sexuality and cultural sophistication. Although we probably don't notice it directly, we are also affected by the dark, rich earth colours in the background – adding to the sense of warmth, seclusion and erotic intimacy. These too are signs that inform our reading.

Most striking (because 'unnatural') is the fact that the woman's nakedness is 'clothed' in light – words (more signs) projected onto her skin. The fact that she is also in the act of writing, creates a dialogue between the two things that gives the image a complex meaning alluded to in the phrases used to promote the film: 'The word is made flesh' and 'Treat me like the page of a book'.

It is disturbing whenever a person is depersonalised, treated like a thing – in this case a canvas or a screen. As an audience, it makes us self-conscious of the fact that she is an object for *us*.

It is the interaction of signs – the juxtaposition of 'nature' and 'artifice', which prompts this sort of interpretation. In a sense, the image *represents* the rather abstract thoughts Greenaway is aiming to stimulate in us. This level of intellectual suggestion is difficult to achieve in film – and rare.

The most important point here, however, is that just looking at the image and responding to it, we are already *doing* semiotics – constructing meaning through interaction with the signs.

EXERCISE

The smallest elements
Take a favourite DVD, select a moment you know well, and pause it.
Now, look for the signs that make up this 'compound image'.
Break it down to its smallest units, and ask what would be different if this, or that, was changed. The difference may be small, but telling. Some changes would create an utterly different film.

The flow of signs

Technically speaking, a 'motion picture' *is* in fact a sequence of individual pictures, but it is *experienced* quite differently – as a steady stream of sensations. A movie is a vast outpouring of signs.

The film-maker's task is to control and channel this flow of information in order to create the desired illusion and shape the audience's experience of it. It is a game of consequences – if I show them *this*, they will think or feel *that*. The way in which you craft and organise your film's signs will determine the reality and meaning an audience will attribute to them.

Changing any one aspect of Peter Greenaway's 'reclining woman' will alter the way the audience perceives her at that moment. If she turns the page they become aware of her as a writer; if she closes her eyes they see her as someone resting or dreaming, if the light moves over her skin they see her as a strange canvas – an aesthetic 'object'. These implications are already there of course, but are re-emphasised by slight changes in the play of signs around her. And changing one thing *can* change *everything*. Just imagine what an accompanying soundtrack of sleazy music would do to the scene.

An audience may not be able to dwell on every single frame of a film but it is extraordinary just how much and how quickly they can process what you give them. Having said this, cinematic images are extraordinarily fleeting. A crucial plot point may occur in a split second. If you overload your audience with too much information, or it comes too quickly, they may single out and concentrate on the wrong thing – miss a crucial element of characterisation or miss a necessary stage in the narrative.

Successful film-making involves keeping the audience 'on track' and pointing them in the right direction throughout – steering their perception and focusing their attention, without seeming to do so.

Glossary

Synecdoche: Where some portion of a thing stands for the whole.

There are some crucial conceptual distinctions that underpin semiotics in its attempt to describe how information is transmitted and received at the most basic level – how meaning is made possible by the 'play of signs' between film-maker and audience.

The two sides of the sign

The first basic insight of semiotics is that a sign has two parts: the physical and the psychological.

- The physical part is the 'sign-as-object', the tangible *thing* we see or hear, such as a metal road sign, the tear in the heroine's eye or the words 'Go for your gun.' This is called 'the signifier' – the external stimulus.

- The psychological part is the 'sign-as-concept', the *reaction* to the object, the mental picture or idea it provokes in the mind. This is called 'the signified' – the internal response to the signifier.

The signifier is what we *perceive* of the sign, while the signified is the actual *meaning* the sign has for us. This distinction between the thing used to communicate (tears) and the thing communicated (sadness), has important implications for film-makers who are trying to effect a precise response in their audience. It is crucial to find the perfect stimulus for the state you want to create *in the viewer*.

The difficulty lies in the fact that the sign has one signifier, but *many* potential signifieds. The signifier is 'out there', fixed and publically shared, whereas the signified is a unique response determined by a range of personal factors. We all interpret things differently according to experience or mood.

What is more, tears *can* be a sign of many things – sorrow, fear, frustration, relief, gratitude, happiness, or a mixture of these. It follows that the relation between signifier and signified is arbitrary. There is no natural bond between the sign-as-perceived and the sign-as-understood. If one character hands another a single red rose the meaning is clear. Yet there is no inherent connection between a garden shrub and romantic love. The link is entirely due to convention – creating an efficient shorthand for quite complex notions that would otherwise require an awful lot of words. In fact, by bypassing language the image creates an emotional attachment to the screen.

Semiotics

Metaphor and metonymy

Metaphor and metonymy are different ways of transmitting meaning. Metaphoric meaning establishes a relationship between two things based on a *resemblance,* sharing a common property, which encourages a *comparison*: 'as quick as a shot', 'as light as a feather', 'my love is like a red, red rose'. Metaphors point to a connection and invite us to elaborate upon it – often imagining something immaterial as if it could be seen or felt.

Metonymic meaning establishes a relationship based on *association* – instead of asserting a resemblance, a metonym *substitutes* one thing with another – 'the bottle' for drink, 'hands' for workers, 'the press' for journalists, 'the crown' for the monarchy, the Oval Office for the US president. As a figure of speech, a metonym replaces numerous changeable things with one single vivid and fixed image (for example 'the pen is mightier than the sword' – meaning words are more effective tools for change than physical violence).

The significance of this for film-makers is that visual texts (unlike literary ones) are characteristically metonymic. In other words, what is seen replaces or substitutes what cannot be seen. Films have difficulty conveying the *experience* of power, wealth or love, but they are good at conveying the trappings and rituals that surround them.

This relationship of part to whole is also very important for film. The technical term for this is **synecdoche**. Our sheriff *is* his badge, our gunslinger *is* his gun. Our heroine *is* a rose – beautiful, but easily crushed. Julia Roberts' character is '*that* smile'. Clint Eastwood's spaghetti Western anti-hero is *that* cigar – smouldering, hard bitten and enduring.

A flag is a metonym – standing for a country or a cause. When D.W. Griffith (*The Birth of a Nation*, 1915) shows a Southern Confederate soldier during the American Civil War ramming a Confederate flag into an enemy cannon, the flag *is* the Confederacy – a brave, romantic, but ultimately futile attempt to resist the mechanised might of the Union army.

Denotation and connotation

A further important distinction exists between two dimensions of meaning – two 'levels of signification':

- **Denotation:** the primary direct 'given' meaning the sign has – e.g. a military uniform and insignia will denote a particular class or rank (private, sergeant, captain, general and so on).

- **Connotation:** the secondary indirect meaning derived from what the sign 'suggests' – for example, military uniforms may connote valour, manliness, oppression, conformity and so on – as the result of collective cultural attitudes or unique personal associations.

Both levels of meaning clearly operate in the still from *The Birth of a Nation* (opposite). Everyone will recognise a hectic battlefield scene and many will recognise the uniform of an officer in the Southern Confederate army during the American Civil War. This is the factually based denotative meaning.

However, the connotations it has, the ideas it evokes, will vary enormously according to the viewer's attitudes to war in general and that war in particular. This leads to another central insight of film semiotics: meaning does not reside *in* the film like some buried treasure awaiting discovery. Meaning is the result of the interaction between the film and the audience – it is a fluctuating process only partially at the film-maker's command. Nevertheless, it is his or her task to exert maximum possible control – to anticipate the range of likely connotations and nudge the audience in the desired direction.

A film is never really good unless the camera is an eye in the head of a poet.

Orson Welles, director, writer, actor and producer

**The Birth of a Nation
(dir: D. W. Griffith 1915)**

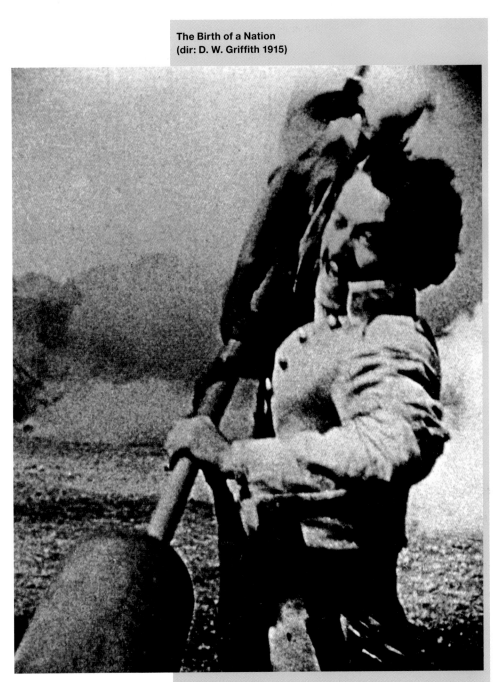

This image of battle sticks in the memory. Whether attacking a cannon with a flag appears courageous, cavalier or just plain crazy – depends, in part, on the way we interpret his ecstatic expression.

In his attempt to discover the essential underlying structure beneath any and all narratives, the French literary theorist **Roland Barthes** identified five separate signifying systems or frameworks through which texts communicate. As we'll explore further in Chapter 2, his analysis is just as relevant and revealing about film, and can help clarify some of the issues of communication that are central to successful film-making.

Five systems of meaning

These systems are referred to as 'codes'. However, this term can be rather misleading and confusing. Barthes *doesn't* mean that film-makers and others are deliberately *adopting* a 'code', which then needs to be *cracked* by some special act of intelligence. What he *is* saying is that narrative artists generate meanings by employing pre-existing structures.

The film-maker doesn't *elect* to use these systems; he or she just decides how to deploy them in a particular situation. They are structures that inevitably come into play the instant anyone starts to organise signs into narrative coherence. Taken together they are to narrative what grammar is to language. They have to be in place for anything to make sense.

Audiences use these conventional systems to construct meaning from texts. None of us need formal training to either encode or decode narrative information in this way – any more than we learned our native language by being told a set of rules or procedures. In both cases, we subconsciously learn as we are immersed in a language-world full of signs and stories.

It may be helpful to re-imagine these 'codes' as five different types of grid, mesh or net in which the signs that make up the text are captured, sifted and meaningfully related one to another. Each net catches different kinds of material; and taken together they constitute a kind of network through which signs are filtered and our perception organised.

Barthes' five codes, or 'systems of meaning', are as follows:

1 **The enigma code**

This is the principal structuring device that sparks the audience's interest and drives a movie forward. All films deliberately set puzzles, pose problems, hint at secrets to be divulged, mysteries to be unravelled, and hopes fulfilled. This is what ignites curiosity, holds attention, and creates suspense and surprise. By withholding and strategically delaying the release of narrative information, film-makers control the audience.

The audience's experience of a movie can be expressed in terms of the almost endless string of questions it prompts us to ask; some implicit, some explicit. Barthes identifies ten types of question – from the initial posing of general questions (What is this going to be about? What's going to happen next?) to the final disclosure at the end (Who did it? Will he get the girl?). He also identified no less than eight different ways to keep the riddle from being solved, including giving partial and multiple answers. In *Psycho* (1960) Alfred Hitchcock, the great master of enigma, uses them all.

2 **The connotative code**

This refers to the signs that imbue characters and settings with meaning, for instance the innumerable sensory signs (speech, clothing, movement or gestures) from which we draw inferences about the characters. These inferences can be complex and subtle, but they all derive from bits of information mentally composed into the illusion of real people having real experiences in a real world.

In watching a movie we note certain connotations (of word or image), which we then organise into themes. For example, as can be seen on page 31, in *Falling Down* Michael Douglas's crew cut, necktie and briefcase constellate into a theme – call it 'responsibility' or 'traditional values' – which places him in a certain relationship with the decayed environment around him.

3 **The action (or proairetic) code**

This refers to signs belonging to the pattern of actions, large or small, that make up the narrative. The most interesting examples tend to show the audience one thing in order to reveal something else. As we've already seen, inner events must be signalled by outer ones if the story is to have human depth. For example, when a cowboy tightens his gunbelt he isn't adjusting his clothing, he is making a life or death decision. When the hero and heroine kiss at the end it is more than a kiss! These actions do not mean what they mean by virtue of our experience of reality, but our exposure to other films.

Glossary

Antitheses: Things or ideas that are opposed to one another.

4 The symbolic code

This relates to the way an audience's reception of texts is determined by organising all experience into a pattern of **antitheses**. These antitheses might include: good/bad; hero/villain; true/false; or life/death. The list is endless, but it is only through this patterning of contrasts that the audience can 'read' the text conceptually, know what it 'means', over and above what merely 'happens'.

Language itself is structured around these binary oppositions and our entire cultural map of beliefs and values is derived from them: right/wrong; rich/poor; master/slave. Not that the pairings are ever strictly equal. In any given context one of the pair of terms is favoured or 'privileged' over the other, reflecting a hierarchy of value. For example, in so far as we sympathise with the central character in *Falling Down* the 'traditional values' he represents are supported and endorsed.

5 The cultural (or referential) code

This encompasses the text's references to things already 'known' and codified by a particular culture. This includes the body of shared assumptions relating to society, such as psychology, morality and politics, without which the world of the text would be unfathomable.

Without a common currency of ideas about the law, marriage and social responsibility we wouldn't understand what *Falling Down* was all about. We don't have to *personally* agree with these ideas, but they operate as a given frame of reference for the struggles the film enacts.

EXERCISE

Reading signs

You don't need to 'take up' semiotics, but Barthes' theory is a useful tool to examine the 'sign-writing' process of movie-making. Now select a favourite scene and use his five-part categorisation to differentiate the signs and your reading of them.

**Falling Down
(dir: Joel Schumacher 1993)**

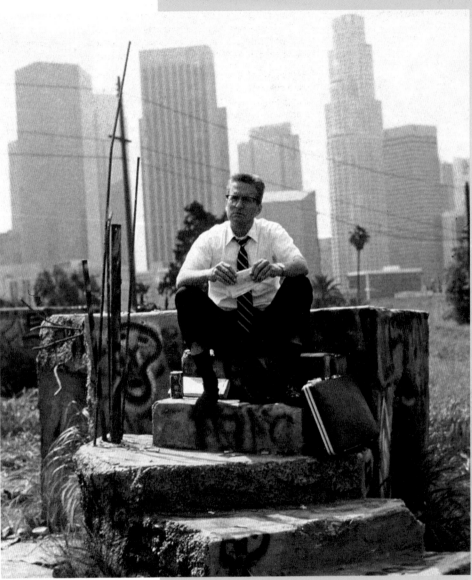

We can use Barthes' five 'codes' to examine Michael Douglas's character: 1) raising questions about how he finds himself in these alien surroundings, 2) defining him by his businesslike appearance, 3) interpreting whether sitting there is an act of fatigue or defiance, 4) exploring the contrast between skyscrapers and demolition sites, and 5) reflecting on the cultural values represented by both.

CASE STUDY

Seven
New Line Cinema

Director | David Fincher

Screenwriter | Andrew Kevin Walker

Cast including | Morgan Freeman (Detective William Somerset)
Brad Pitt (Detective David Mills)
Kevin Spacey (John Doe)
Gwyneth Paltrow (Tracy Mills)

Crew including | Darius Khondji (cinematography)
Richard Francis-Bruce (editing)
Arthur Max (production design)
Gary Wissner (art director)

Tagline | Seven deadly sins, seven ways to die.

Seven
(dir: David Fincher 1995)

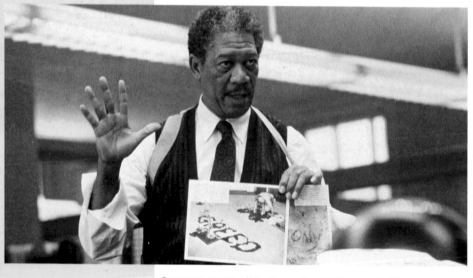

Somerset counts off the Seven Deadly Sins, and holds up a message from the killer which carries the signature 'idea' behind these apparently motiveless crimes. It is delivered in the form of a sign which only Somerset can 'read' and truly understand.

Synopsis

Police Detective Somerset is counting down the last seven days before his retirement. Called to investigate a suspicious death he detects the work of a serial killer who chooses victims to represent the Seven Deadly Sins. Knowing it will be a long-running investigation Somerset is reluctant to be involved. However, he is equally sure that Mills, a young cop new to the city's homicide unit, is not yet ready for this kind of job.

Roland Barthes' five codes are clearly in operation in every part of David Fincher's *Seven*. Like any film – but perhaps more than most – this taut pitch-black thriller is a swirling sea of signs. The central conceit of the movie invites a semiotic analysis, as it seems to hinge on the ability to decipher a cryptic message. Even the title itself plays with systems of meaning. A great deal of the film's publicity refers to it as *Se7en*.

Key connotations

The moment it begins the movie sets us to work, dealing out bits of information that the viewer can sort into appropriate patterns of understanding. Our senses are on maximum alert for the 'road signs' that signal the kind of experience the film is going to give us.

The 'world' of the film is created with great economy. Before anything appears on the screen we hear distant wailing sirens summoning up associations of danger and rescue, criminality and law enforcement. The almost constant rain adds an element of claustrophobia to the background hostility and menace of the soundtrack.

This external environment contrasts with the first visual images we see, as we follow Somerset (Morgan Freeman) moving slowly around the hushed and dimly lit interior of his apartment, getting prepared to face the city streets. His calm and methodical manner conveys an inner stillness, which will be his hallmark.

Recommended viewing

Watch the opening of Steven Spielberg's *Schindler's List* (1993) for another example of a character 'getting dressed' for the benefit of the audience.

Tip

When introducing a central character find an excuse to linger on them doing something indicative of who and what they are.

Things to look out for

Somerset in the library. What semiotics attach to poker, books and Bach?

Assembly

In these early scenes, Somerset is being 'assembled' for us from a series of carefully chosen outward signs that inform the audience who he is and what to expect from him. He tidies his kitchen, and one by one collects the personal effects neatly lined up on his dressing table. He carefully places a fountain pen in the pocket of his crisp white shirt, and plucks fluff from his suit.

When we next see him he looks like the stereotypical American detective complete with trench coat and trilby – a costume that adds to his air of authority, but singles him out as a figure slightly displaced in time.

The chess set in the foreground of the opening shot suggests intellectual combat and a struggle between black and white – good and evil. The switchblade he later throws with such shocking force and deadly accuracy into a dartboard represents mental sharpness, directness and efficiency.

Other objects associated with Somerset represent extensions of his personality. When we see him in his cramped office pecking away at an old-fashioned manual typewriter we are seeing someone comfortably self-contained in his working habits, but 'out of step' with modern ways. He says as much: 'I don't understand this place any more.'

Most striking of all is the metronome that he keeps beside his bed. Its regular motion reflects the order he craves and drowns out the chaos that encroaches from the street outside. These noises – emergency vehicles and angry voices, are the world he lives in and wishes to escape.

All these signs point to Somerset's psychology – to the qualities of intelligence and calculation, maturity and independence, moderation and self-control, which equip him for the task ahead. They are visible-external-signifiers of the invisible-internal-signified – his *mind*. These signs give the illusion of human depth and complexity that makes him 'real' to us, and allow us to attribute to him beliefs and desires that can then go unstated. Creating a coherent character profile encourages the audience to feel they recognise and understand him. Attaching to him they attach to the film.

Working the enigmas

Being a detective thriller the whole movie is explicitly structured around the need to solve a mystery. We are already alert to the overriding question the film asks. Who is behind these murders? Why 'seven'? Where are the clues that will lead them to him? These question marks take us further and further into the heart of the film. One of the audacious things about this movie is the explicit way it foregrounds the 'breadcrumb' procedure of clues and guesswork, which is the staple of the detective story.

Not only do we have the implicit countdown through the seven days of the week, but we see Somerset being seduced into investigating the case. Although he is determined to avoid involvement, his boss cunningly piques his interest – putting evidence on his desk (thin slithers of linoleum taken from the gluttony victim's stomach), and quietly mentioning over his shoulder as he leaves: 'They were fed to him.' Somerset is also being fed a line – and he bites. Somerset's curiosity gets the better of him. He's hooked, and so are we.

This trail of breadcrumbs orientates the audience towards closure and the ultimate satisfaction of 'order restored'. Nevertheless, the big punch line delivered at the end of *Seven*, and the sudden change of direction implied by the words 'I'll be around' leave us with something both shocking and thought-provoking.

Actions speak louder than words

We experience something strangely familiar when we follow Somerset back to the crime scene. Hearing a strange throbbing coming from the refrigerator, he turns to find not only where the plastic came from but the note from the murderer that confirms his worst fears. Somerset here exhibits the powers of observation and intuition we associate with a master sleuth. He is on the villain's wavelength, with special insight into his deranged mind, and a methodical approach that cuts out all extraneous or superfluous influences. When he flatly refuses the coffee which his new partner Mills offers him on the way to the victim's apartment, it shows him to be intent only on the job at hand.

Recommended viewing

Watch the opening of Steven Spielberg's *Schindler's List* (1993) for another example of a character 'getting dressed' for the benefit of the audience.

Tip

When introducing a central character find an excuse to linger on them doing something indicative of who and what they are.

Things to look out for

Somerset in the library. What semiotics attach to poker, books and Bach?

Codes and filters > **Case study: Seven**

Glossary

Motif: A dominant idea or concept, a recurring formal element, colour or design feature. Repeated use of a particular shot distance can be developed into a motif through repetition and variation.

The clash of opposites

Barthes' symbolic code offers the richest vein for analysis. The 'cut' from the sound of Somerset's metronome to the edgy credit sequence juxtaposes order and chaos, method and madness in a way that perfectly captures the conceptual polarity around which the entire film turns.

Somerset and Mills embody a pattern of oppositions too numerous to mention. They belong to the time-honoured tradition of the buddy movie – chalk and cheese, brains and brawn, the ever-steady and the unstable – a relationship beginning in hostility, but ending in mutual respect. We read each according to the other.

Their sharpest opposition appears in the cross-cutting between the library where Somerset has gone to do research on the Seven Deadly Sins and damnation, while Mills sits at home fruitlessly studying the files. The engraved illustrations depicting Hell in the copies of Dante's *Purgatorio* and Milton's *Paradise Lost* not only resemble the twisted corpses in the crime photographs, but reflect Mills' tortured incomprehension. Lacking the 'culture' Somerset and John Doe share, Mills simply cannot read the signs.

When we see his wife looking on through a veil curtain, her role as angelic witness is clear. She is also the bridge that will bring the two men together.

Cultural code

In order to understand even the first few minutes of the movie (including the edgy relationship between Somerset and Mills, their interview with the Captain, Mills' wife's reference to 'tracker poles', and so on) the audience needs to understand a host of commonly held assumptions relating to personal ambition, seniority of status, professional advancement, career structures, hierarchies of responsibility, the authority of experience, and more. In other words, the audience needs to recognise (if not necessarily share) the values that dominate the modern world. An entire social structure is implied.

And of course, to understand the central **motif** of the film the audience must be able to *recognise* a host of moral and religious ideas based on a distinction between 'crimes' that break the law of man – and acts that offend Almighty God. In a culture where such a distinction did not exist, the film would not only lack the frisson of Hell and eternal damnation – we would hardly understand it at all.

**Seven
(dir: David Fincher 1995)**

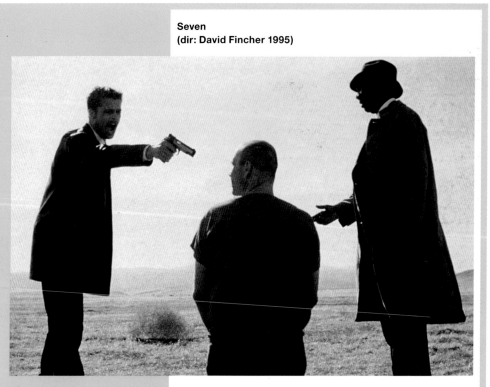

Seven takes us into moral and philosophical territory, and conducts a debate about human nature and social responsibility – it is the movie's innumerable signs that lead us there.

DISCUSSION QUESTIONS

Seven is an amalgam of signs and uses the familiar 'myth' of the Seven Deadly Sins as the backbone of the story. What other signs are in operation to let you know you are watching a thriller?

Seven asks a number of questions (enigmas); consider what they are for you and where they appear in the film.

Unusually, *Seven* ends with an enigma. Do you think Mills shoots the killer?

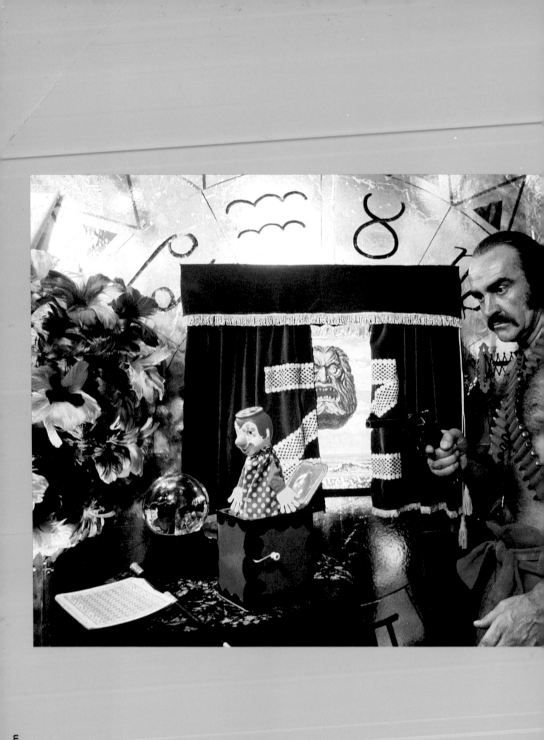

NARRATIVE

Zardoz
(dir: John Boorman 1973)

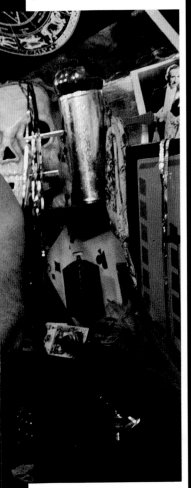

The first thing to be considered in film analysis and production is the complexity of the overarching narrative structure. This implies that narrative is about stories. On one level it is, but narrative analysis is about much more than that. Narrative analysis is the study of the specifics of communication as it relates to structure – the details of the language that film uses.

As if that didn't sound complex enough, narrative is further complicated by its relationship to the real world. Film has its own specific language and as such is unconnected to reality in the way we might assume it is. However, as an audience, we have to believe that what we are seeing is real. It is the complexity of the relationship of narrative elements to narrative wholes and the relationship of both of these to the 'real world' that makes narrative so fiendish for analysis and complex for film-makers. Either way, you need to understand your medium.

Zardoz is an interesting film depicting a society based around myth and legend – and therefore based around narratives. In the end, it is a copy of *The Wizard of Oz* that leads Zed to understand the world he inhabits. It is also both interesting and terrifying because of Sean Connery's costume.

It was Frank S. Mottershaw's *A Daring Daylight Burglary* in 1903 that heralded a new vision for the moving picture as he introduced fictional storytelling to the medium. As part of the Sheffield Photo Company, Mottershaw pioneered a number of what would now be referred to as action films. The techniques that these films established quickly spread across the world and were further developed, most notably in Hollywood.

The film-maker as theorist

This new form of storytelling included numerous scenes, cameras were placed carefully, and editing, particularly cutting on action, was introduced. From these techniques genres were established. This early foray into narrative-based cinema began to define the language of film. This is now as familiar to us as any spoken or written language. Like other languages it appears natural, but the language film uses is as carefully constructed and contextually driven as any other.

Film theory has its esoteric elements, which are often highly divorced from the practice of cinema, but on the whole it interrogates meaning, communication and audience reaction. The vocabulary adopted by film theory may sometimes seem distant from the practice of making a film – the ideas certainly are not. Many great film-makers are often the best (informal) students of their own medium and can talk eloquently about their own art and the work of film-makers they admire. They are aware of the tools of meaning and communication and employ them as second nature.

For the new film-maker, a sound knowledge of theory can lift your craft and turn it into art. It can also speed up a process, aid effective communication with a crew and improve precision.

The theorist as film-maker

The worst kind of theorist is one who takes no account of the context of film production; who sees film as nothing more than literature or history with moving pictures. To ignore the context in which a film is made and received is to disregard one of the things that makes film so special.

A working knowledge of the process of producing film is therefore helpful for the film theorist. Knowledge of shot types, how sound is recorded, how a crew really work together, the realities of having to use available footage in post-production, and so on, is essential information. This doesn't mean that every film theorist should leap out of their chair and grab a camera; much of this can be gleaned from observation or from reading about the experiences of directors. One thing that digital technology does afford the theorist is the opportunity to begin to engage in the process of production. Testing out ideas, shot types and so on is both enjoyable and informative, even if you have no ambition to ever make a film.

The audience

The majority of film theory, and a great deal of this book, is about the audience. Too often audiences are forgotten when film is treated as film, as an entity that exists almost divorced from any point of reception. Film is nothing without an audience. Like theatre, film is designed for an audience; it is meaningless without them. Film theory forces the audience back into the equation. Audiences are varied and contingent, but it is important that we at least acknowledge they exist.

Structuralism

Glossary

Text: A verbal, written or visual artefact. Film is a medium that combines all these elements and thus the complexity of analysis is increased.

Recommended reading

Aristotle's *Poetics* (c. 335 BCE) is the foundation of all narrative analysis; it is thought-provoking and surprisingly accessible. Roland Barthes' *An Introduction to the Structural Analysis of Narratives* (1965) will help you put the specific filmic theories on narrative into a broader context.

Structuralism is an umbrella term for many different movements that share approaches to the analysis of the world. In structuralism's terms, everything in the world is available as '**text**' and can be analysed in the same terms. Text thus means everything is available for analysis by the same set of broad principles. A text such as *Mythologies* (Roland Barthes, 1957) exemplifies this where Barthes uses the rules of structuralism and semiotics to analyse wrestling, red wine and print media all in the same terms. This is the basis of film analysis.

Structuralism for film-makers

Structuralism developed out of the linguistic analysis of Ferdinand de Saussure (1857–1913) and in particular his book *Course in General Linguistics* (published posthumously in 1916). His principles were taken, developed and applied to all aspects of human interaction to become the movement we understand today as structuralism. Film has its own specific language and as such the theories of a movement based in the study of language are particularly pertinent.

The benefits of a working knowledge of structuralism and its branches of semiotics and narratology are evident for film theorists. The advantages for the film-maker are less obvious, but no less vital. Most film-makers are hugely knowledgeable about the form they work in; be it the cinema history of Martin Scorsese or the avant-garde artistic expression of Derek Jarman. Film-makers tend not to use the vocabulary of structuralism, but they implicitly use the approaches. When you are starting out you should endeavour to use both. Structuralism, as the name suggests, is about structure, and the smallest elements that go together to make up structure; this means that it can be used to ensure precision.

There have been many developments from structuralism such as post-structuralism and deconstruction, which challenge the assumptions made in the original theory. However it is important to note two things:

1 Without knowledge of structuralist principles it is impossible to engage in subsequent debates.

2 Film language does not evolve in the same way as spoken language – it is a highly structured form.

The foundation of narrative analysis

The study of narrative in film has been examined in a great deal of depth by a wide range of theorists and practitioners in a variety of different academic fields. Film narrative has been studied, appropriated and used by sociologists, psychologists, cultural theorists, anthropologists and semioticians as well as by literary theorists. However, by far the most plentiful source of narrative analysis has come from academics with a literary background who often work under the assumption that all narratives operate in the same way.

Much of the narrative analysis that film theory purports to have developed comes via the structuralist revolution of the 1960s; a theoretical system that still maintains much of its base in Aristotle's *Poetics*, which essentially deals with drama rather than literature or film.

If you string together a set of speeches expressive of character, and well finished in point and diction and thought, you will not produce the essential tragic effect nearly so well as with a play which, however deficient in these respects, yet has a plot and artistically constructed incidents.

Aristotle, *Poetics*

Structural analysis

In his *An Introduction to the Structural Analysis of Narratives* (1965)
Roland Barthes made many clear and compelling connections
between narrative and the real world. Four of the key points to
remember are:

1 Narratives appear in many forms: written, verbal and visual –
   all of which form part of the complex language of cinema.

2 Narratives are constructed, they don't just appear; they are selected
   and ordered. This is true of real life, but we do this on a subconscious
   level. In film it is deliberate.

3 Narratives apply to all human and cultural interaction – narrative
   discourse operates throughout all culture and throughout all time.
   This in itself makes the relationship between the real world and a film
   world even more complex for analysis, but it also allows the maker
   a great deal of freedom.

4 Narratives are 'transhistorical' – they have always existed and by
   implication always will. This implies that narrative is primordial. In
   these terms film is now part of the real world – film language is yet
   another language that we engage with on a regular basis.

This is the basis of narrative analysis in cinema – that there are
comparisons between day-to-day communication and film language.
However, film has its own specific modes of communication. It is the
intersection between everyday life and film form that creates meaning
for an audience. This suggests something fundamental.

Narrative is not the same as story; that is too simplistic. Narrative
is about comprehension. Narrative is a fundamental facet of human
communication.

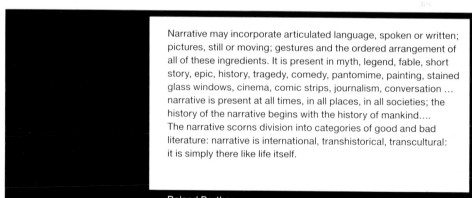

Narrative may incorporate articulated language, spoken or written;
pictures, still or moving; gestures and the ordered arrangement of
all of these ingredients. It is present in myth, legend, fable, short
story, epic, history, tragedy, comedy, pantomime, painting, stained
glass windows, cinema, comic strips, journalism, conversation …
narrative is present at all times, in all places, in all societies; the
history of the narrative begins with the history of mankind….
The narrative scorns division into categories of good and bad
literature: narrative is international, transhistorical, transcultural:
it is simply there like life itself.

Roland Barthes,
An Introduction to the Structural Analysis of Narratives, 1965

Narrative

Narratology

Narratology is the name given to the study of narrative and narrative structure. In looking for patterns and trends in all texts it is part of the structuralist movement. This grouping of thinkers is informed by Saussure, but also by Claude Lévi-Strauss who (as a structural anthropologist) looked at repetitive narrative structures across different countries and cultures. In these terms, film narratology is concerned with both language (as in film's specific codes and conventions) and context and often the relationship between the two.

Story and plot

We have established that narrative is about much, much more than simply telling stories, but in terms of filmic narratives meaning starts to be generated when plot is established. In unpicking a film or setting out to create a film, it is possible to start with an overarching story but the plot has to follow quickly in order for things to make sense.

This is essentially because plot is about causality – how one event or action leads to another. If this is not made explicit then a film makes no sense at all. As E. M. Forster said: '*The king died and then the queen died* is a story. *The king died, and then the queen died of grief* is a plot.' If this is not established by the film-maker then an audience will try and establish it themselves.

EXERCISE

Finding the plot
Take the key elements of any well-known film of your choice and write them down as bullet points. Avoid noting the causal relationships and then present this to three or four different people – can they identify the film? Then, try adding in a couple of the actual plot points, noting the different narratives that emerge. Once you have added these plot points you should show the breakdown to the same group of people and assess how many of them can identify the film from this simple breakdown.

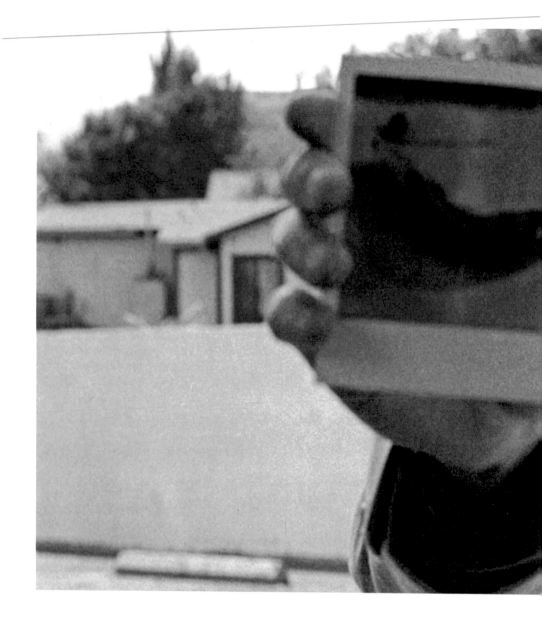

**Memento
(dir: Christopher Nolan 2000)**

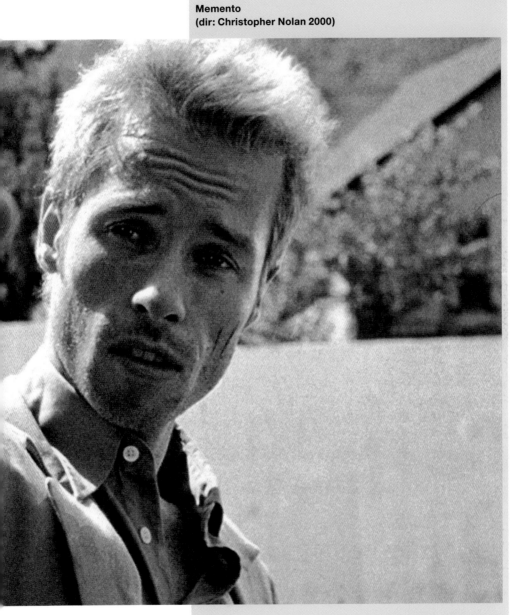

Memento is an interesting film on a number of levels; in this instance because of its casual relationships. It was lauded as a film that experiments with narrative. This is not the case. It is a film that clearly reverses the narrative. Part of the quest for the audience is to piece together the relationship between events. This is still conventional narrative form.

Recommended reading

It would be valuable to read *The Screenwriter's Workbook* (2006) by Syd Field. Field has his detractors and his supporters but regardless of your opinion his work provokes thought about the rigidity of structure in Hollywood cinema.

Structure is vital. This seems like an obvious statement, but budding film-makers often think that a good structure will naturally emerge from a good story rather than being set out from the start. The temptation is also to assume that structure is the preserve of the screenwriter. While the writer undoubtedly is the first person to deal with structure, and has to be aware of the forms in which they are working, structure is an essential consideration for all members of the team. Developing a unified structure for your film will require the cooperation of everyone involved in the production.

The formalists and Vladimir Propp

The formalists, or Russian formalists, worked between 1910 and 1930. They are significant in their detailed concern for the nature of poetic language. The Russian formalists looked to the nature of 'art' in its broadest sense and were keen proponents of avant-garde work. One key member aligned to the formalists was Vladimir Propp.

Propp developed the *Morphology of the Folk Tale* in 1928, although this didn't have a broad Western impact until the late 1950s and as such became an early part of narratological analysis. Propp's work is well-trodden ground, but worth returning to as its impact cannot be underestimated.

Propp categorised the characters that appear in folk tales as 'The Seven Spheres of Action':

1 Villain
2 Helper
3 Donor (often magician)
4 Female in distress and her father
5 Dispatcher
6 Hero
7 False hero

Propp's work has been developed for film analysis by people such as Will Wright in his book *Sixguns and Society: A Structural Study of the Western* (1977), which examines narrative patterns in the Western. Wright uses Propp's theories and lists directly. Since then, many criticisms have been levelled against Propp's work. In some ways, this is hugely unfair as Propp never claimed that his rules could be used for anything other than the folk tale. The argument follows that any film could be made to fit the lists on pages 50–51; it is an exercise worth trying. The question that comes from this is whether the lists presented by theorists such as Propp are reductionist in the way they compress the structure and content of a film into such a simple form. In analysis this depends on the type of film itself. Some films are made to reach as wide an audience as possible, and as such may use a simple structure, and the most simple and familiar is that analysed by Propp. The film-maker may be using their own knowledge of the fairy tale; the analyst will be using the framework presented by Propp.

EXERCISE

Reading fairy tales

Try picking a film that bears the traits of the folk tale or fairy tale and see how it fits into The Seven Spheres of Action. A film such as *Star Wars* is too obvious and has been done. Then attempt the same process with a film such as *Schindler's List* (dir: Steven Spielberg 1993) and then something like *Week End* (dir: Jean Luc Godard 1967). The results may be very interesting. From this you can debate why Godard's work is labelled avant-garde and why Spielberg came under some criticism for *Schindler's List*, despite laudable attempts to represent the horror of the Holocaust. Some of these criticisms focused on the need to have Schindler as the 'hero' rather than a Jewish character, and other feelings of emotional exploitation.

Propp's narrative elements

The following list is how Vladimir Propp defined the progression of a fairy tale – the narrative elements. He claimed that not all elements had to be used in every story, but many would be.

1 A member of a family leaves home (the hero is introduced);

2 An interdiction is addressed to the hero ('don't go there', 'go to this place');

3 The interdiction is violated (villain enters the tale);

4 The villain makes an attempt at reconnaissance (either villain tries to find the children/jewels etc.; or intended victim questions the villain);

5 The villain gains information about the victim;

6 The villain attempts to deceive the victim and take possession of victim or victim's belongings (trickery; villain disguised, tries to win confidence of victim);

7 Victim taken in by deception, unwittingly helping the enemy;

8 Villain causes harm/injury to family member (by abduction, theft of magical agent, spoiling crops, plunders in other forms, causes a disappearance, expels someone, casts spell on someone, substitutes child etc., commits murder, imprisons/detains someone, threatens forced marriage, provides nightly torments); alternatively, a member of family lacks something or desires something (magical potion etc.);

9 Misfortune or lack is made known (hero is dispatched, hears call for help etc.; alternative is that victimised hero is sent away, freed from imprisonment);

10 Seeker agrees to, or decides upon counter-action;

11 Hero leaves home;

12 Hero is tested, interrogated, attacked etc., preparing the way for his/her receiving magical agent or helper (donor);

13 Hero reacts to actions of future donor (withstands/ fails the test, frees captive, reconciles disputants, performs service, uses adversary's powers against them);

14 Hero acquires use of a magical agent (directly transferred, located, purchased, prepared, spontaneously appears, eaten/drunk, help offered by other characters);

15 Hero is transferred, delivered or led to whereabouts of an object of the search;

16 Hero and villain join in direct combat;

17 Hero is branded (wounded/ marked, receives ring or scarf);

18 Villain is defeated (killed in combat, defeated in contest, killed while asleep, banished);

19 Initial misfortune or lack is resolved (object of search distributed, spell broken, slain person revived, captive freed);

20 Hero returns;

21 Hero is pursued (pursuer tries to kill, eat, undermine the hero);

22 Hero is rescued from pursuit (obstacles delay pursuer, hero hides or is hidden, hero transforms unrecognisably, hero saved from attempt on his/her life);

23 Hero unrecognised, arrives home or in another country;

24 False hero presents unfounded claims;

25 Difficult task proposed to the hero (trial by ordeal, riddles, test of strength/ endurance, other tasks);

26 Task is resolved;

27 Hero is recognised (by mark, brand, or item given to him/her);

28 False hero or villain is exposed;

29 Hero is given a new appearance (is made whole, handsome, given new garments etc.);

30 Villain is punished;

31 Hero marries and ascends the throne (is rewarded/promoted).

EXERCISE

Using Propp
Take your idea for a film and pit it against Propp's character list and sequencing list. How far does this help you in forcing a narrative sequence and plot development?

Glossary

Surrealism: A short-lived artistic movement that sought to explore subjective dream-states and was concerned with subverting the logic of representation. It is often incorrectly used today to refer to things that are unusual.

The classic Hollywood narrative structure

Tzvetan Todorov developed Propp's notions and boiled them down even further to try and identify the barest elements of narrative structure. Todorov developed his notions of how narrative communication works during the early part of his career and these structuralist principles informed much of his analysis in the 1970s and into the 1980s. His narrative sequencing started with three elements that built on Aristotle's notion of structure.

Equilibrium (beginning) → Disruption of equilibrium (middle) → Return to equilibrium (end)

Todorov expanded this to involve the characters, to offer a recognisable reason for the initial three stages:

1 Equilibrium is established.
2 Disruption to the equilibrium.
3 Character(s) identify the disruption.
4 Characters seek to resolve the issue to solve the problem to restore equilibrium.
5 Reinstatement of equilibrium.

This is a useful aide-memoire, even if you are attempting to create a non-narrative form. In attempting to do this you cannot create something wholly random. Audiences expect narrative sequences – this is part of the language of cinema that has been established. If you want to challenge an audience the first place to start might be to play with this sequence.

A note on non-narrative forms

Be very careful when setting out to create something which is non-narrative. There is a world of difference between something that is abstract and something that 'plays' with narrative form. The former tends to be video art or some of the more extreme examples of **surrealism** (such as *Un Chien Andalou* (dir: Luis Bunuel 1929). Other film-makers who tend towards experimentation utilise an audience's knowledge of narrative structure and convention, for example Hal Hartley's short *Ambition* (1991).

The classic Hollywood three-act structure

The classic Hollywood narrative sequence has been developed since the conception of Hollywood as the dominant seat of production. In these terms, it has become part of the vocabulary of cinema not because it is 'natural' but because it has been repeated.

Syd Field is one of the most respected screenwriting gurus working in America. Field identified the following structure and suggested its use for all other film-makers. For Field, the three key stages of any film are: setup, confrontation and resolution. These are broken down as follows:

Act 1 Comprises the first quarter of the screenplay.
In a 120-minute film Act 1 = 30 minutes.

Act 2 The next two quarters of the film.
In a 120-minute film Act 2 = 60 minutes.

Act 3 The final quarter of the film.
In a 120-minute film Act 3 = 30 minutes.

Recommended viewing

There are many films worth examining to investigate Hollywood structure. A film such as *The Apartment* (dir: Billy Wilder 1960) is a classic. An interesting exercise is to compare and contrast the structure of Hollywood remakes, such as *Boudu, sauvé des eaux* (dir: Jean Renoir 1932) and *Down and Out in Beverley Hills* (dir: Paul Mazursky 1986).

Aristotle's *Poetics*

As we've already seen, Aristotle's *Poetics* is the foundation of all criticism and theory as we understand it today. In it he defines the barest elements of narrative:

'A whole is that which has beginning, middle and end. A beginning is that which is not itself necessarily after anything else, and which has naturally something else after it; an end is that which is naturally after something itself, either as its necessary or usual consequent, and with nothing else after it; and a middle, that which is by nature after one thing and also before another.'

While this seems so obvious that it is almost pointless stating it, this is to misread Aristotle. *Poetics* is a treatise on the nature of drama and what Aristotle is pointing out is that the narrative sequencing resulting in a beginning, a middle and an end is a construction born out of the desire to make drama coherent. This is then distinct from everyday communication, where the requirement for narrative completion is not the same – everyday life doesn't have such neat beginnings, middles and ends.

Gérard Genette's *Narrative Discourse: An Essay in Method* (1983) is intended for all narratives in all modes. For this reason, Genette's is the most comprehensive narratology available and it is his connection of narrative and discourse that is most important of all. In these terms discourse can be defined as the imparting of knowledge and, most essentially, debate.

Story (Content)

Events	chronology/causality
Characters	actions/interactions
Settings	spatio-temporal complexes

Narration (Telling)

Types	reliable/unreliable
Levels	embedded narration
Voice	narrator/character

Text (Presentation)

Time	order/duration/frequency
Characterisation	traits/attributes
Focalisation	who sees/perceives/judges events?

In *Narrative Discourse* Genette examines a number of essential points. He does not purport to provide structure, as Propp does, or to oversimplify structure as with Todorov or Field. Instead he identifies the key elements in narrative; elements that have to be present in order for a narrative to make sense. More than this he identifies the key elements that make a narrative mean something to an audience.

With the introduction of the element of 'text' he identified how meaning is not down to the decision-making faculties of an audience. This is not directly the same as the ideology identified and discussed in Chapter 4, instead this is the buried and subsumed meaning that is generated from the structure of the specific narrative form.

Story

Story is the primary level of any narrative. This is the section that the inexperienced film-maker starts and finishes with. The inexperienced critic does the same. This is where the content is developed and meaning begins, but this is not how meaning is communicated. Genette posits that events, characters and settings need to be treated with particular consideration:

Events: things happen, but it is crucial to note the causal relationships. In these terms events become a plot.

Characters: there are characters who interact with each other (interactions) and they do things (actions). This is not the same as characterisation. This is crucial because a character that does not really do anything, or doesn't progress the plot, becomes part of the setting.

Setting: things happen and characters exist in a particular time and place. This frames the characters and the events.

This then provides the starting point for developing the content, but doesn't touch on form in any great detail.

Narration

As a narratologist, Genette is concerned with all narratives and as such his levels of narration are highly detailed. Speech is often overlooked in production and analysis. Who is speaking, when, where and to whom are all vital questions. When placed against how we view characters this becomes even more complicated. The notion of reliability is paramount. If we have seen a character behaving in a duplicitous manner we are unlikely to believe what they are saying. Where characters are consistent we are unlikely to question what they say. This even stretches to the morally ambiguous detectives in film noir.

The positioning of narration is an important consideration and in cinema it can be separated into three main areas:

Extradiegetic: narration from an exterior voice, not a character in the film, or where we don't know who the character is at that stage. A voice-over. The first few seconds of The Apartment (dir: Billy Wilder 1960) exemplifies this.

Homodiegetic: a character narrator. A voice-over or the rare example of a character speaking directly to camera. For instance, the opening dialogue from Lester Burham in American Beauty (dir: Sam Mendes 1999).

Intradiegetic: two or more characters speaking to each other – remember they speak to further characterisation and/or plot, not for their own benefit.

Theories of structure > Genette's narrative discourse > Music

**Forrest Gump
(dir: Robert Zemeckis 1994)**

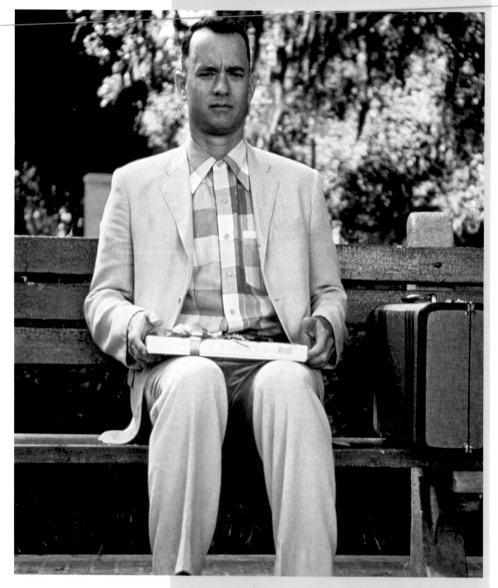

Forrest Gump contains all three forms of narration; intradiegetic (for example, when Gump is talking to the woman on the bench), extradiegetic (where no character is in shot or the viewer sees things that Gump cannot have seen) and homodiegetic (where we see Gump in shot talking about himself). Sometimes all three of these techniques are used within a single scene.

Making meaning – text

It is Genette's category of 'text' that is of most importance to the budding film-maker and the considered critic. This is the section where meaning is generated for an audience. This is the manipulative phase. For an analyst, this is the aspect of the film to delve into. For the film-maker, this is the aspect to prioritise.

Characterisation: this helps characters become real for an audience. It is their traits and attributes, as if they were real people.

Time: this refers to characters, settings, actions; in fact all of the elements of narrative outlined above. The simplest way to consider this is in relation to repetition; the more we see things the more likely it is to stick. More than this, it is the order in which we see things and how long they last. All of these things will go to aid our prioritisation of particular aspects of a film narrative.

Focalisation: this is the final and crucial positioning of an audience. This is where the viewpoint of a character takes priority and dominance. This doesn't mean that a character needs lots of information or even as much information as us. It is about viewpoint rather than knowledge.

François Jost and ocularisation

François Jost's concept of 'ocularisation' is interesting to the prospective film-maker because it relates directly to the prioritisation of the image:

'To distinguish the relationship between how the camera shows the hero and how the hero is supposed to be seen, I propose to speak of *ocularisation*. In effect, this term is valuable in evoking the field of action taken by the camera. When it sees things from the position of the character this is 'internal ocularisation': when the opposite occurs whereby it sees things from the position of some other person, I have provisionally used the term *external ocularisation*.'

François Jost – 'Narration(s): en deçà et au-delà', Communications, 38, 1983 (my translation).

By this Jost means that the position of the camera with, or alongside, the protagonist shifts the audience's attention to that position.

It is worth looking at the films of particular *auteurs* to establish whether the music plays a part in our familiarity with their work. For example, Woody Allen's use of familiar jazz tracks or Alfred Hitchcock's recurrent use of Bernard Herrman.

Music cannot directly communicate narrative in the same way that dialogue can. However, it can provide a backdrop to visual events and dialogue and it is this subtlety that may position an audience in a way that dialogue cannot. Music is representative and emotive. It can engage an audience at a different level and capture their emotions rather than their conscious mind. It is difficult to avoid the emotive pull of a well-executed score.

Ways of working with music

There is one mode of storytelling that exists in cinema beyond that of showing and telling: music. This facet of cinema can have a dramatic effect on character. Music can impact on our emotions and as such can limit what emotional impact a scene has upon us; and this is different in every film. It doesn't matter whether it is the incidental music, a popular soundtrack or a themed score; it all affects us as an audience. This use of music has been treated by theorists as an aspect of narration, but it cannot tell, it can merely aid focalisation in relation to that which is being shown and told by affecting mood. This is the aspect of film that acts as a backdrop and some film-makers, such as Ingmar Bergman, feel it should not be included as it clearly breaks with presentation of both characters and events in terms of relating them directly to the real world.

Whatever the use of music is within any film it is complex to identify its precise meaning – such is the nature of music. However, to ignore it is to ignore a powerful part of the signifying practice of cinema.

EXERCISE

Manipulating sound
Redubbing a film is always an interesting exercise. In doing this you can see how the replacement of, say, a specific score with tangentially related popular music tracks fundamentally impacts on your ability to 'read' the film, even down to the point of being able to view who the main characters are and what they do.

**Manhunter
(dir: Michael Mann 1986)**

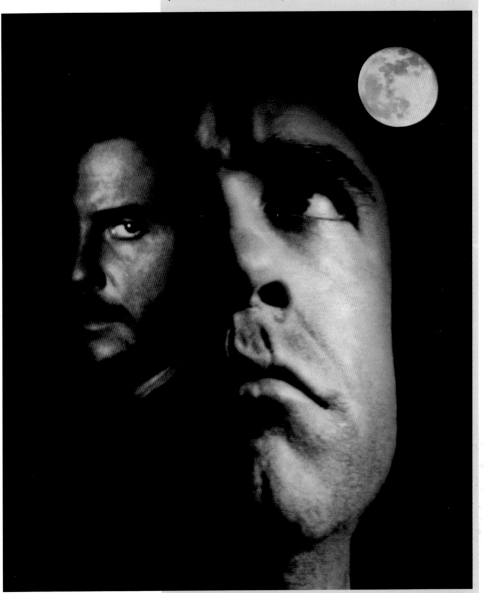

There are many sequences in *Manhunter* where the soundtrack dominates the film. The music is supposed to heighten the audience's reaction to the onscreen action but is not sufficiently subtle and so becomes a distraction. Instead of drawing the viewer in, the music actually distances the viewer from the storytelling.

Genette's narrative discourse > **Music** > Case study: Cheap Beans

CASE STUDY

Cheap Beans
Lithium Heart Productions/York St John University

Director	Martyn Johnston
Screenwriter	Martyn Johnston
Producer	Rachel Higgins
Cast including	Ben Hepworth (Man) Faye Knight (Woman)
Crew including	Matt Allsop (cinematography) Bethan Clancy (editing) Lauren Agar (production design) Will Standish (sound and music)
Tagline	He was hungry – for love.

Synopsis

Take a look at the short film *Cheap Beans* (2008) – available at www.avabooks.ch/index.php/ava/bookdetails/978-2-940411-27-6. The film opens with an unnamed man living in a squalid apartment. He goes out to buy cheap baked beans and sees his dream partner – the woman working on the checkout. He strives to make contact by reinventing himself to become like the people he sees her chatting to – but embarrasses himself in his efforts to impress her. As he leaves the supermarket he sees her boyfriend; a person who is essentially a carbon copy of himself before he tried to change.

The specifics of short film

There are some aspects of short film production and reception that differ substantially from feature films. It is worth studying these differences prior to either beginning work on your own short film or analysing the work of others. First, it's worth noting that the actual language of film is not dependent on the length of the film, it is the way in which the narrative is constructed and communicated that differs. Overarching narratives are therefore the same as features, but the specifics are different.

Generally speaking this means that short films tend to have:

- Only a few characters – who are characterised in detail, and thus possibly more characters who are not characterised, who are there as part of the setting.

- No subplots.

- Fewer settings/locations.

- Cuts between major plot points.

Obviously, these factors are all dictated by the length of the film, but the net result is that short film can have a different character from feature films and it is important to recognise the similarities and the differences.

Cheap Beans: The title sequence

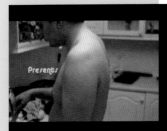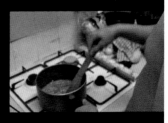

This title sequence begins the process of establishing character. The loner in the squalid flat is clear and unambiguous and his low income is emphasised by the title of the film, underscored with the images of beans.

Story and plot

Cheap Beans has a deceptively simple structure. This is common amongst short films. In a sense, short films do often have a simpler structure than features in that they contain little extraneous detail. This does not necessarily make them any easier to work with. In fact there are many more complexities in the process of *reading* the language due to this lack of detail. *Cheap Beans* is based on a simple 'boy meets girl' story. In some senses this aligns itself to the romantic comedy genre and thus audiences come to the film with expectations. This, however, is not the full story; that would be too easy. In fact, this is a 'boy meets girl, doesn't get girl, but could have got girl' story. If there is a message it is perhaps: 'be yourself'. In this sense, the story concerns itself with the events that progress the narrative and the characters that support this.

Cheap Beans: The meeting

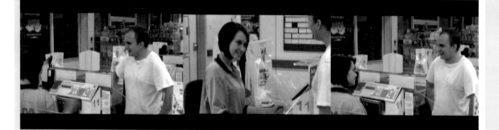

The meeting between the two main protagonists is carefully staged. This is where his kindly yet insecure traits are established. It is important that he sees her first, yet there is evidence of initial attraction, otherwise his quest for her would make no sense; she thus makes clear eye contact.

Plot is about the connections between these aspects of the story. As short films tend to be character driven, it is the characters that progress the narrative. As a general rule, short films don't tend to leap around between locations and *Cheap Beans* is no exception. It has two locations and the characters exist and, most importantly, function between these two. The plot is driven by the motivation of the central character. This is built by the insecurity outlined in being attracted to the cashier and then feeling undercut by the other customers. It is our protagonist's sight of the other customers and then his decision to change his behaviour in relation to how he views them that provides the plot. This is simple and yet it is still a plot – it is still the aspect that links the elements.

Three acts?

While Hollywood films tend towards a neat three-act structure, as outlined by Syd Field, short films don't have the 90 to 120 minutes outlined in his theory. But they do still have a structure. The structure of *Cheap Beans* is built into acts that take on board Todorov's conception of the dramatic narrative. There is much less time allowed for this than in a feature film, however, and not just because of the restricted running time of the film. Short film audiences tend to be far more interested in the middle section of the narrative – the disruption to the equilibrium and the hero's quest to restore the equilibrium, than they are in the initial set-up.

- Equilibrium (beginning): Man alone at home cooking beans, buys more beans, sees woman – 1m 14s.
- Disruption of equilibrium (middle): Man tries to attain woman.
- Return to equilibrium (end): Man realises he has no money and thus has failed in his romantic quest – 11m 25s.

Cheap Beans is a good example of a film where the equilibrium is ultimately restored. Although this doesn't mean that the ending is positive – the main protagonist is left alone and thus not too happy. However, this is where he started, so equilibrium is restored. This gives us the twist at the ending; after all the trouble he has gone to it turns out that her boyfriend is just the same as him. If he hadn't tried to change his appearance it could have been him. It also gives the audience a resolution. This exemplifies an important point: resolution is for the audience, not necessarily for the characters.

Text

As we've seen, according to Gérard Genette (page 54), text is where meaning is really generated. In *Cheap Beans* the text breaks down as follows:

Time (order/duration/frequency): as with a great deal of good comedy, *Cheap Beans* is built on repetition. The repetition builds the joke and propels the narrative. However, there is much more than that to the film's use of order, duration and frequency in narrative terms. The opening takes in the protagonist's apartment slowly and carefully and then does the same with the supermarket. This is important as the action then moves to a close-up of the protagonist getting dressed and the checkout. This establishment is important as it is not repeated. The repetition is built through the stream of characters that pass through the checkout, and it is this (accompanied by the beeping till) that builds the plot.

Characterisation (traits/attributes): the characters are established in the first moment we see them. The cashier is clearly a cashier, she is sitting in the right place and wearing the right uniform. Our hero is established via his apartment, his clothes and his actions. These in turn point to his personality traits and he is quickly established as something of a slob. In short films it is important to establish the protagonists' characteristics quickly and efficiently. In *Cheap Beans*, the protagonist's key characteristic is insecurity, shown through his inability to act on his attraction to the cashier when he believes she is attracted to other characters. This insecurity is endearing and makes an otherwise unpleasant character one the audience will want to follow.

Focalisation (who sees/perceives/judges events?): as the only character who is characterised in any real detail *Cheap Beans* establishes the man as the focaliser in the opening scene. While the opening is not viewed from the character's perspective, it establishes the view of the apartment that he would have. The view of the supermarket features him in the centre of the frame and the view of the cashier is his and his alone. His suspicion that she is flirting with other customers is emphasised and supported by the close-ups of the actions and interactions at the checkout.

Cheap Beans: The competition

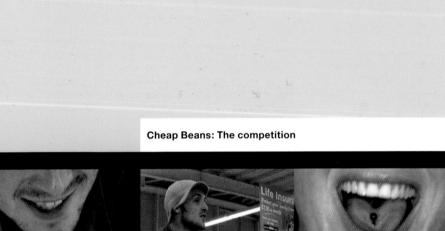

The main protagonist must be unnerved by what he sees and as
he is the focaliser the image on the screen is refracted through
his eyes, or at least his viewpoint. It is thus important that the
handsome customer is the antithesis of everything he is. The
close-ups of mouths add a dimension of sensuality that has been
lacking until that point and is bound to enrage him.

Narration, sound and music

Cheap Beans is a silent film. It bears many of the hallmarks of silent film in connoting meaning by using close-ups on people's faces to provide clues to emotion, and clear and slightly exaggerated action. Narration is all about telling – the most direct and, in many ways, easiest method of communicating meaning. (Ironically, constructing dialogue is often the hardest part of the screenwriters' craft.) *Cheap Beans* still communicates effectively and well.

The meaning of the piece and the narrative sequence is developed through the visuals and is supported by the much more intangible aspects of sound and music. The music fulfils the conventions of silent cinema; it is familiar to an audience as being of that particular form and as such carries the joviality and history of the medium. This is crucial for an audience as the film could never be a real tragedy – despite the ending and the continued isolation of the person that we have come to empathise with.

It is worth remembering that no sound used in film is 'real'; it is all there for a reason and is selected and constructed in the same way as all other aspects of narrative and film form. The Foley sound (the sounds that synchronise with what's on screen, such as footsteps) in *Cheap Beans* works in terms of Genette's conception of 'text' and the subcategory of 'time'. The sound is sparse but pointed and as such takes on more importance. This is best exemplified via the moments of high sexual tension in the last sequence at the checkout. The beeps emphasise and heighten the tension. They work with the associated close-ups of faces and hands; all these things give the scene a very particular rhythm.

What this demonstrates is that while we might prioritise the visual image as the primary mode of storytelling used by cinema as an audience, as analysts we have to take account of the auditory power it has. As potential film-makers, it is important to note how much power sound has, this is the part of cinema that can be the most subtle in its manipulation of an audience.

Cheap Beans: The ending

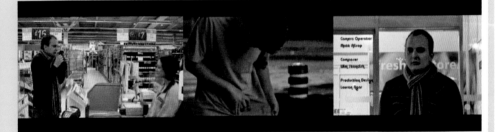

The ending moves from the familiar light to the darkness outside, furthering the idea that this is an ending. The sight of the mouths noted in earlier scenes are echoed here allowing us the belief and hope that he may win. Of course, he does not and instead sees his doppelganger outside; the tragedy plays out.

DISCUSSION QUESTIONS

Compare *Cheap Beans* to any similar humorous feature film. For you, what are the fundamental differences in plot?

Sound can create emotion; this is particularly true of a silent film. How is the music here constructed to underline what we see?

The end of *Cheap Beans* is clear, but does this work with or against our expectations?

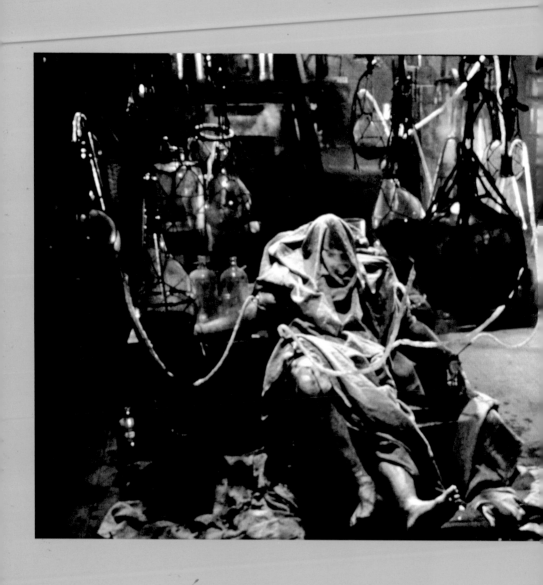

INTERTEXTUALITY

**Frankenstein
(dir: Kenneth Branagh 1994)**

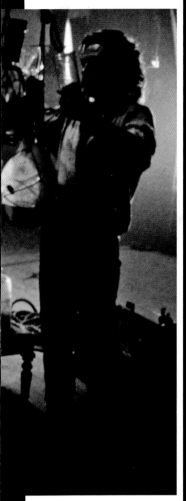

Films are not created in a vacuum. They emerge from a cinematic tradition and are produced within a social context that thoroughly informs both the film and its reception.

Like other forms of storytelling, movie-making requires little in the way of pure invention. It generally entails the careful assembly and grafting together of pre-existing elements. Every film is supported by a standard batch of vital organs – old myths, familiar character types and well-worn narrative conventions, all re-animated (hopefully) by an individual bolt of creative lightning.

Luckily, we are surrounded by a vast body of material from which to harvest what we need. Knowingly or not, the latest blockbuster owes its existence to this resource. The general term for this relationship is 'intertextuality'.

Every film-maker is a
Dr Frankenstein, creating
a new body from existing parts.
Each movie is a patchwork of
tissue taken from other movies.
Only be sure you know where
the pieces come from and
the effect they will have –
and don't leave the best bits
on the cutting-room floor!

Glossary

Intertextuality: The shaping of one text by other texts – the interrelationship between texts.

Film is a cultural product. It does not grow, it is built. The camera may reproduce the appearance of real objects, but a movie is an artificial construct, a 'text', a body of discourse (words and images) based on principles born of history and convention. In Chapter 1 we looked at some of these conventional practices, and revealed how any film can be viewed as a mosaic of signs. However, semiotics is just one aspect of the intertextual nature of cinema.

The body of the text

It would appear that from earliest times people have made the connection between texts and textiles. Storytellers are said to spin a yarn and weave the fabric of a tale. Audiences are drawn into the story, follow (or lose) the thread, see (or not) an emerging pattern. Plots are said to become knotted and get untangled – to zigzag, crisscross, wind to a close, and reveal a final twist.

This metaphor is deeply embedded in our language. It suggests that a text is a tapestry woven from many intertwining strands, and that a film-maker's task is to select this 'stuff' and tie it into a tight and coherent whole. A text is like a quilt of disparate fragments cunningly stitched together to make something arresting and unique. This analogy is central to a great deal of modern theoretical thought.

The term **intertextuality** was first introduced by Julia Kristeva in the late 1960s. She sought to assert that the meaning we find in a text is not to be located in its relationship to the mind in which it seems to have originated, but in its relationship to *other texts*. In a very real sense texts have a life of their own, enabling, inspiring and generating each other. Film begets film.

These thoughts of Kristeva's build in turn on earlier ideas about language derived from another theorist, Mikhail Bakhtin. He suggested that all human communication is dialogic – meaning that every utterance is a contribution to an ongoing dialogue. Every word reflects what has gone before, and is shaped by anticipation of how it will be received.

Cinema, too, is dialogic. Any film refers (however obliquely) to other films, and is a response to them. What is more, the meaning a particular film has for an audience is determined by its relationship to this textual background. We read a film in the light of its resemblance to other films, and the associations (conscious or otherwise) it has for us. As a film-maker you need to engage deliberately in this 'conversation with the familiar', and ensure as far as possible that the connections viewers make are consistent with your intentions.

Bodysnatching?

As we saw in Chapter 1 (pages 32–37), intertextuality is *explicitly* at work in David Fincher's *Seven*. Other texts and contexts imported from theology, psychoanalysis, literature, painting, and classical music, as well as film, are easy to spot on its surface. David Fincher is not cheating.

All films tap into a shared cultural heritage and emerge from a web of pre-existing materials and expressive forms.

Intertextuality is not theft – it is the inevitable state of all art. Any film builds on (and from) what has gone before. This may sound rather uninspired, and uninspiring, but the 'artistry' is in making something that strikes an audience as new and distinct.

Far from limiting originality, the 'restriction' of working within a set of conventions can be genuinely liberating. Not only is there a wealth of ready-made ideas to play with, but genre provides a backdrop against which tiny individual touches are thrown into sharper relief and take on a disproportionate significance.

The bigger picture

Intertextuality is not confined to the impact of one text on another. It cannot be reduced entirely to a simple matter of original sources. Nor are we always referring to direct influence and conscious imitation.

Of course, ideas *do* get copied or recycled for obvious commercial reasons. One successful comic book movie will spawn another, and then another, until the novelty wears off and the profits diminish. But this is in part a natural consequence of the social contexts from which movies arise. The ever-vigilant and mysterious 'caped crusader' is an appropriate fantasy in an age when *real* terror invisibly stalks our city streets.

Larger-than-life images from books and films get traded back and forth – in playground games and newspaper columns, in coffee shop discussions and classroom debates, until they become the staple currency of our thought. They reflect the anxieties and issues that preoccupy us. The media pick them up and use them as a sort of shorthand.

Figures such as *Wall Street*'s (dir: John McTiernan 1989) Gordon Gekko and *Die Hard*'s (dir: Oliver Stone 1988) John McClane have fallen into the collective imagination as concentrated personifications of unscrupulous greed and determined heroism. They have become part of our cultural landscape – their characters and catchphrases encapsulating attitudes towards unfettered capitalism and terrorist threats, which continue to shape contemporary reality.

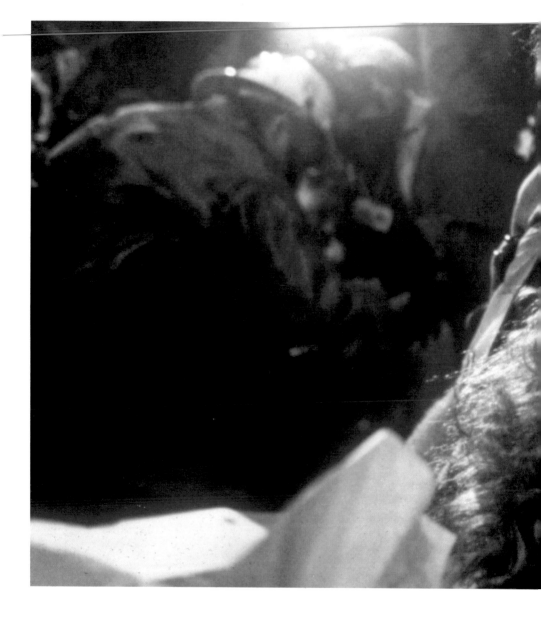

**Die Hard
(dir: John McTiernan 1988)**

Films emerge from and contribute to the all-embracing text
we call 'culture'. In the *Die Hard* films, Bruce Willis's wry-smiling,
no-nonsense character protects everything he loves from a host
of international villains. The character both reflects and reinforces
the idea of the lone all-American hero that has been a part of
US culture since the days of the *The Lone Ranger* in the 1930s.

Text > Quotation

Recommended reading

Robert Stam, *New Vocabularies in Film Semiotics* (1992) – this theoretical book offers a history of film theory, defines over 500 critical terms and describes how they have been used.

Films can interact with one another in a wide variety of ways and on many different levels. Some intertextual references are conscious and deliberate, with one film directly pointing to another. These references fall into two broad categories: quotation and allusion. Let's start by looking at some of the forms of quotation.

Appropriation

The most overt form of quotation is the appropriation of one text by another. This sort of 'cut and paste' incorporation of pre-existing material is relatively rare, but very instructive. For instance, in the background to Terry Gilliam's dystopian sci-fi satire *Brazil* (1985), we glimpse government employees secretly viewing snatches of the movie *Casablanca* (dir: Michael Curtiz 1942). This classic wartime story represents all the action and romance that the central protagonist Sam Lowry and his co-workers crave amid their bureaucratically controlled lives. Sam's fantasies of flying away with the woman he loves are both fuelled and mocked by the comparison.

This is also the case in Woody Allen's comedy, *Play It Again, Sam* (1972), which actually opens by showing *Casablanca*'s dramatic finale. As the propellers whirr into life and the celebrated climax plays out, the camera pulls back and we see Woody's awestruck face looking up at the cinema screen mouthing the famous concluding lines.

Thereafter, Humphrey Bogart's tough-guy persona (played by Jerry Lacy) pops up from time to time offering Woody somewhat anachronistic advice on being a 'guy' and getting a 'dame'. The question of whether escapist fantasies and fictional role models are a help or a hindrance is an integral part of the film's more serious purpose. *Play It Again, Sam* pays homage to a great film of the past *and* offers a telling comment on the distance between cinematic experience and real life.

Play It Again, Sam goes so far as to follow the plot of *Casablanca*, ending in a re-enactment of the opening scene, in which Woody gets to *be* Humph. The effect of this cinematic borrowing is that something of the original aura of *Casablanca* is transferred to the later movie, creating a special bond with the audience and importing a wealth of intellectual and emotional associations that we and Woody 'share'.

Another Woody Allen film, *Zelig* (1983), takes appropriation still further. The film follows the history of a nondescript little man with a chameleon-like ability to transform his appearance and melt into his surroundings. As the cinematic equivalent of his psychological condition, Woody's character is magically inserted into archive newsreel footage, at one point sharing a balcony with Adolf Hitler.

These self-referential games strongly appeal to film-makers and audiences alike. They tease the imagination and raise questions about the status of the 'reality' we are viewing. The illusion is at once both doubled and dismantled in the act of showing us 'the miracle of film'.

The interpenetration of texts gives a peculiar pleasure that has to do with the momentary revelation of their true nature – that they are the material consequence of selection and arrangement, and are themselves fragments of the immense unfolding cultural tapestry we live in.

Tip

Examine your most recent film ideas, and try to identify the directors or specific films you are consciously or unconsciously in dialogue with. Your relationship to them is already shaping your thoughts and aims.

**Play It Again, Sam
(dir: Herbert Ross 1972)**

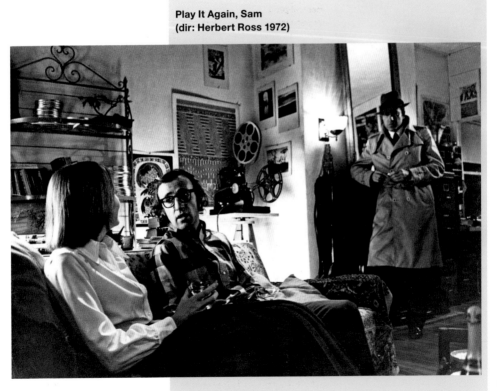

Casablanca represents the high-water mark of a certain brand of romantic escapism. It inevitably stands in the shadows behind any movie that seeks to occupy the same territory.

Great popular films haunt both the imagination of movie-goers *and* the movie-making that follows them. Invoked or not, Bogart is there.

Text > **Quotation** > Allusion

Tip

Think about a specific piece of pre-recorded music you would ideally like to use for a particular scene. Not only will the music shape the orchestration of the action, but import qualities which must complement rather than detract from your visual intentions. Identify what these are.

Dialogue

Textual quotation is not restricted to other films. In *Seven* we not only have the illustrated books Somerset consults in the library – paintings by Hieronymus Bosch and Albrecht Dürer, woodcuts of Biblical scenes from Genesis and the Book of Revelation, and illustrations of episodes in Dante's *Divine Comedy* and Milton's *Paradise Lost* – but their full significance is only rendered in contrast to yet another text: a recording of orchestral music by J. S. Bach, as sober, dignified and balanced as the visual images are twisted and deformed. Texts talk to one another.

Such references invite the age-old debate over whether the angelic or demonic in mankind will prevail. The film's own ambivalent answer comes in a response to a quotation taken from Ernest Hemingway's novel *For Whom the Bell Tolls* (1940). In this way intertextuality creates a link to otherwise remote ideas and issues, and connects the movie with the cultural database already loaded into the audience. By means of drawing on other texts and discourses, meanings are redoubled and amplified, and a modern thriller takes on a timeless resonance.

Although such *overt* referencing of other texts *is* relatively uncommon, it stands as a conspicuous example of something that is actually happening all the time. Texts are constantly coinciding and overlapping on the screen and in our minds. The meaning of every angelic smile and demonic glare is seen against the dense intertextual background that makes up our shared cultural memory.

Scream 2 (dir: Wes Craven 1997) 'foregrounds' this background, so to speak – not only parodying horror films in general, but commenting ironically on its own previous incarnation. When characters attend a movie based on the events of the first *Scream* film and later discuss the 'rules' of a horror *sequel*, the swirl of in-jokes and self-reference is an integral part of the fun.

> ...any text is constructed of a mosaic of quotations;
> any text is the absorption and transformation of another.

Julia Kristeva, philospher and literary critic

**Scream 2
(dir: Wes Craven 1997)**

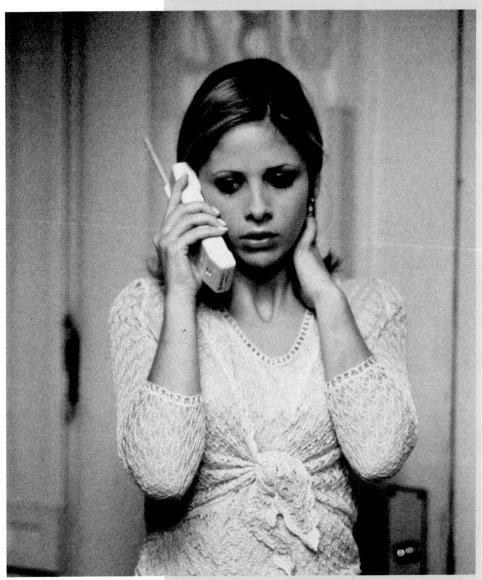

Here we see Sarah Michelle Gellar in the 'film within a film' at
the beginning of *Scream 2* – recreating the role played by Drew
Barrymore in the first film. This ironic playfulness is significant
in the development of the language of film; intertextual references
have always been there, now film-makers can make them obvious –
if they want to.

Whereas quotation involves some kind of duplication in which other material is reproduced and embedded, allusion involves a verbal or visual *evocation* of another movie – relying on the audience to make the connection. There are numerous ways in which one film can allude to another. Here are just four:

Reference

The title of the film *The Usual Suspects* (dir: Bryan Singer 1995) derives from a famous line in *Casablanca*, where Captain Renault of the Vichy Police is ordering the rounding-up of known criminal elements in a pretence of activity intended to impress the Nazi SS. Obviously this (literal) quotation is intended to sound a familiar note and pick up some reflected glory. Nevertheless, the phrase has significance in itself – referring to the cunning smokescreen erected at the centre of Bryan Singer's darkly labyrinthine plot. The police line-up which became the dominant publicity image, ironically conceals the film's narrative complexity.

References can also be visual. For example, *Brazil* (dir: Terry Gilliam 1985) is one of numerous films to re-enact the famous scene in Sergei M. Eisenstein's *Battleship Potemkin* (1925) where a baby carriage bounces down the seemingly endless Odessa Steps. Citing this iconic example of montage technique is a respectful nod from one director to another, and a backward wink to those in the audience who know their film history. The mental nudge towards this famous image of state repression, Tsarist Cossacks massacring innocent civilians, endorses the serious message behind Gilliam's political satire.

Self-reference

Some movies cannibalise *themselves*. For example, films in the Harry Potter franchise constantly reflect back on previous events, not only to bring us up to date with a long and complex story but to cement our nostalgic attachment to the children's younger selves. The same comforting air of familiarity is a central appeal of sequels in general.

EXERCISE

Refashioning
Select a favourite film moment that you could imagine recreating in your own movie. Ask yourself how you would refashion it to fit your purpose. This may reveal a lot about the general tone and style you should be adopting throughout.

Association

Other allusions are far less explicit, like those carried from one film to another by an actor. For instance, any director choosing to cast Anthony Perkins after 1961 was deliberately importing some of his notorious performance as Norman Bates in *Psycho*. His portrayal of a neurotically disturbed misfit left an indelible trace that was impossible to ignore or erase.

You can see him stuttering and twitching his way through *Murder on the Orient Express* (dir: Sidney Lumet 1974), where he plays (you guessed it) a young man with a fixation on an older woman. At one point in this Agatha Christie murder mystery we see the back of a tall figure dressed in a kimono sashaying down the corridor of a train. The film-maker is teasing the sophisticated film-goer who will naturally suspect (incorrectly, as it turns out) that Perkins is 'doing a Norman'.

Other associations may derive from the subject matter. The final sequence of *Brazil* incorporates numerous echoes, which compete with one another to form the film's defining note. The abseiling resistance fighters echo the armed assault on the evil mastermind's stronghold that concludes almost every Bond film, while Sam's medical trauma might remind us of *One Flew Over the Cuckoo's Nest* (dir: Milos Forman 1975) or *Kiss of the Spider Woman* (dir: Hector Babenco 1985).

Such associations set up conflicting hopes and expectations, which are less than resolved when Sam is heard murmuring the film's bitter-sweet theme tune. We, the audience, are left to decide precisely where Sam is, and where else we would wish him to be. These same thoughts cluster around almost every dystopian fantasy including those mentioned in the following pages.

Style

In adopting certain cinematic techniques and stylistic features, one film-maker may allude to the work of another. So Woody Allen *does* Ingmar Bergman and Brian de Palma *does* Alfred Hitchcock – acknowledging indebtedness, but also inviting invidious comparisons.

Tip

Think carefully about the 'ideal' casting for your movie. This will tell you a lot about your central characters, and what you need *your* actor to bring to the part.

Intertextuality operates freely in popular culture, and especially in the sort of popular films that acquire cult status. Indeed much of their success may be due to the way they plug into something much larger then themselves; a world that fans and enthusiasts can explore independently. Let's take a look at some classic examples:

Star Wars

Star Wars (dir: George Lucas 1977) borrows heavily from other textual worlds. For example, the Jedi can be seen as an order of medieval warrior knights wielding swords of light instead of metal. Luke is a young King Arthur, and Obi-Wan Kenobi his Merlin. Han Solo is a brash Lancelot, and Princess Leia a feisty Guinevere – until we discover why marrying Arthur is quite out of the question! On another (perhaps less conscious) level R2-D2 and C-3PO are a bickering Laurel and Hardy double act; one twittering but endearing, the other pompous and bossy.

More specifically the narrative point of view and the use of frame wipes as transitional devices were directly inspired by an Akira Kurosawa film, *The Hidden Fortress* (1958). Whereas the climax, the pinpoint attack on the weak spot in the Death Star's defences, is influenced by British war films such as *The Dam Busters* (dir: Michael Anderson 1955) and *633 Squadron* (dir: Walter Grauman 1964).

But the deepest influence on the film (and arguably the source of its unparalleled popularity) is the work of the scholar Joseph Campbell, whose comparison of ancient mythology in *The Hero With a Thousand Faces* (1949) describes a universal spiritual journey – a psychological initiation of trial and empowerment, which underwrites what some regard as Lucas's own modern myth.

Blade Runner

Possibly the greatest sci-fi movie ever made, *Blade Runner* (dir: Ridley Scott 1982), is a modern re-working of Mary Shelley's novel *Frankenstein* (1818). *Blade Runner*'s 'mad scientist' (Tyrell) has made a whole class of beings, known as replicants, now in search of their creator. Whereas Mary Shelley's 'Monster' was a failed experiment cast out because of his brute ugliness, Ridley Scott's robotic life forms are threatening precisely because they are perfect, and perfectly indistinguishable from the human beings they crave to be.

The Matrix

The futuristic chic of *Blade Runner* also inspired the dystopian vision of *The Matrix* (dir: Andy and Larry Wachowski 1999), which is a veritable encyclopaedia of literary, cinematic and cultural intertextuality.

Verbal allusion is made to *Alice in Wonderland* (1865) and *The Wizard of Oz* (1900), while the movie's eye-catching violence upgrades the 'bullet ballets' of director Sam Peckinpah and the martial arts movies of Bruce Lee. The world of liquid pods owes something to the rings of Hell in Dante's *Divine Comedy*, while the simulated reality of the Matrix itself is an infinitely expanded version of the *Star Trek* 'holodeck'.

A great deal of the film's glamour comes from associations outside movie-dom. *The Matrix* is full of references to religion (oracles, messianic Christianity, Zen Buddhism), philosophy (Plato's Allegory of the Cave, Descartes' deceiving demon, thought experiments about brains in vats) and modern anxieties about the internet, cyberspace and virtual reality.

These (and many other) associations lend gravitas to the film's glossy surface, and flatter the audience that can recognise and play with these abstract ideas. If we know our Plato or Lewis Carroll, the text immeasurably expands in significance. If we spot the references to other films, we feel included in a way that rewards our attention and keeps us engaged long after the movie is over.

The Matrix
(dir: Andy and Larry Wachowski 1999)

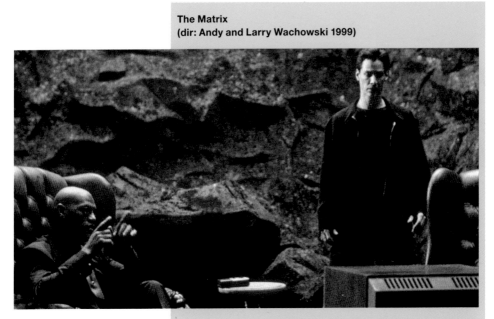

The whole concept of 'The Desert of the Real' (shown here) derives from two books: Aldous Huxley's futuristic satire *Brave New World* (1932) and Jean Baudrillard's *Simulacra and Simulation* (1985), a book that literally appears at the beginning of the film when Neo uses it to hide his illicit software.

Allusion > **Cult film** > Genre

Primary plots

Some movies are straightforwardly based on other texts. *Casablanca* is a film adaptation of an unpublished stage play entitled *Everybody Comes to Rick's* by Murray Burnett and Joan Alison, and *Blade Runner* actually adapts Philip K. Dick's novel *Do Androids Dream of Electric Sheep?* (1968). Similarly, films such as *Ghandi* (dir: Richard Attenborough 1982), *Titanic* (dir: James Cameron 1997) and *Saving Private Ryan* (dir: Steven Spielberg 1998) have their origin in real documented events.

But even more fundamental than literary or historical sources are primary story-patterns; these are the narrative foundations upon which all stories are built. These primary plots reflect the basic experiences of every human life – we grow up, face challenges, go on adventures, face various temptations, win things, lose things, fall in and out of love. These are human universals – hence our interest in seeing them acted out in books and films. Tapping into this common core of experience, a film-maker is engaging with an audience in a potentially powerful way.

The suggestion that the infinite abundance of narrative is generated from a few basic plots may seem unlikely, but it bears the test. As we saw in Chapter 2, precisely what these stories are is a subject of debate, but with a certain amount of imagination any film can be described in one or more of the terms in the box opposite.

Watching old movies is like spending an evening with those people next door. They bore us, and we wouldn't go out of our way to see them; we drop in on them because they're so close. If it took some effort to see old movies, we might try to find out which were the good ones, and if people saw only the good ones maybe they would still respect old movies. As it is, people sit and watch movies that audiences walked out on thirty years ago. Like Lot's wife, we are tempted to take another look, attracted not by evil but by something that seems much more shameful – our own innocence.

Pauline Kael, film critic

Seven primary plots

Achilles: stories of overcoming. However mighty, the central protagonist must have a weak spot, their 'Achilles' heel', which by making them vulnerable humanises them. Think Superman and his kryptonite.

Cinderella: stories of transformation. However lowly and unpromising, the character can rise up and reveal their true nature. Think *Rocky* (dir: John G. Avildsen 1976) and *Pretty Woman* (dir: Garry Marshall 1990).

Jason: stories of pursuit. However meagre, difficult or improbable the quest, the character must attempt it. Think *Thelma and Louise* (dir: Ridley Scott 1991), *The Lord of the Rings* (dir: Peter Jackson 2001) and every detective story.

Faust: stories of temptation. However absurd the bargain, the character will risk everything and put themselves in the hands of another. Think *Wall Street* (dir: Oliver Stone 1987) and *The Terminator* (dir: James Cameron 1984).

Orpheus: stories of irrevocable loss. However long or hazardous the voyage, the hero must undertake a perilous journey to retrieve what they have lost. Think *Regarding Henry* (dir: Mike Nichols 1991) and *Memento* (dir: Christopher Nolan 2000).

Romeo and Juliet: stories of love triumphant. Boy and girl meet, overcome obstacles and come together (somehow). Think *Sleepless in Seattle* (dir: Nora Ephron 1993) and *Moonstruck* (dir: Norman Jewison 1987).

Tristan and Isolde: stories of love defeated. Boy and girl meet, but one of them is already taken. Think *Now Voyager* (dir: Irving Rapper 1942) and *Fatal Attraction* (dir: Adrian Lyne 1987).

When we talk of science-fiction films, gangster pictures, detective thrillers, disaster movies and biopics we are referring to different **genres**. When we speak more specifically of *romantic* comedies, *screwball* comedies, *political* thrillers and *alien invasion* movies we are referring to **sub-genres** – subsets of genre. Looking at genre means looking at the way texts get categorised into types or classes, and the significance this has for film-makers and audiences alike.

Industry branding

The film industry uses genre as a mode of classification, a way of labelling their product and positioning it in the marketplace. The concept of genre helps to create and feed the cinema-goer's appetite for certain sorts of 'product' as it helps them to personally identify with this or that sort of film. A movie can then be targeted at a particular constituent audience. Success can never be guaranteed, but thinking in terms of genre is one way of maximising satisfaction, spotting trends and responding to changing tastes.

Audiences are elusive, fickle and demanding. On the one hand, they generally want to know what they are getting, and genre categories provide the orientation they need to steer them in that direction. On the other hand, they want to be surprised by something more than the standard generic product. Audiences want the same, but different.

Audiences can never come to a new film with an entirely open mind or neutral attitude. Their anticipation levels are already set by pre-conceived ideas concerning the genre to which *this* movie belongs. They ready themselves for the sort of attention it will require, the level of reality they are entering, and the degree to which they will need to suspend their disbelief. They then measure the sort of experience they are having against others they have already had.

It is important to understand the audience's preconceptions and expectations, with a view to meeting, exceeding or subverting them. These expectations relate to both aesthetics and narrative.

Intertextuality

An aesthetic category

A genre is a collection of instantly recognisable stylistic features. No strict definition of a particular genre is possible, but the words 'musical', 'thriller' and 'courtroom drama' immediately conjure up a fairly limited repertoire of ideas: a physical environment; typical locations; the look of the characters, significant objects and so on. Just naming a genre evokes a particular range of surface features belonging to that family of films.

The Western is a cinematic world all of its own composed of Stetsons, horses, saloons, marshals, guns and gunfights usually set within the surrounding of the wilderness of 19th-century America. It is a genre form tied inexorably to a particular historical past – just as science fiction is tied to notions of the future. In contrast, a romance can take place anytime, anywhere – wearing any clothes (or none at all) – because what defines a romance is the nature of the story, not the qualities of the world it occurs in.

A narrative category

Genre is also a narrative category carrying distinctive structural features, certain kinds of story, varieties of character relationship and typical patterns of character development. When we recognise the genre, we anticipate being taken on a particular kind of journey. This climate of expectation allows for certain experiences, but not others – *these* things can happen, *these* can't. The limits are set by genre.

It's OK for gangsters to quote scripture and have in-depth discussions about cheeseburgers – as happens in *Pulp Fiction* (dir: Quentin Tarantino 1994), but they can't lift buildings. It's fine for superheroes to lift buildings and see through walls (as in *Superman* dir: Richard Donner 1978), but they can't turn back time – or if they do it has to be using the perfectly reasonable method of spinning the Earth backwards!

It *is* acceptable for wizards, given the right magical spell, to turn back time – think *Harry Potter and the Prisoner of Azkaban* (dir: Alfonso Cuarón 2004), but going into outer space would be preposterous and *wrong*. Hermione Granger's 'time-turner' is utterly logical within the world she and the audience inhabit.

These design limits are essential because if *everything* was possible *nothing* could be surprising. Genre places an envelope around the story, an envelope that can be pushed, but should not burst. If it does, the viewer is lost, and any sense of 'reality' evaporates. Genre identity preserves the film's integrity; you lose it at your peril.

Genre blending

Although films that lack genre definition, which slip between categories, are less likely to get made, it is also true that movies that cross or straddle genres can often prove the most successful. *Star Wars* is essentially a 'coming of age' Western set in space. *Blade Runner* is a psychological, noir detective, sci-fi thriller. *The Matrix* is all these, and more.

According to the theorist Umberto Eco the unparalleled popularity of *Casablanca* is due in no small measure to the fact that it contains elements of almost *every* genre – being a wartime espionage-thriller romance-comedy buddy-movie – with the real 'horror' of the Third Reich (and a few songs) thrown in. Basically, it delivers what you want no matter what you want. It is all things to all viewers. Genres can happily cohabit as long as they don't interfere with one another.

Casablanca is not just one film. It is many films, an anthology.... When all the archetypes burst in shamelessly, we reach Homeric depths. Two clichés make us laugh. A hundred clichés move us. For we sense dimly that the clichés are talking *among themselves*, and celebrating a reunion.

Umberto Eco, philosopher, literary critic and novelist

Intertextuality

Genre bending

In Terry Gilliam's *Brazil*, different genres deliberately clash to create very surprising effects. The movie's playfulness is announced at the very outset when a caption tells the audience the exact time of day: 8.49 pm, followed by the vaguest reference to 'Somewhere in the 20th Century'.

Stylistically, the film continues to mix the precise and the indeterminate. The action takes place in a totalitarian future, but one that has the fashions and manners of 1930s Britain. The technology manages to be both advanced and primitive; flat-screen computers attached to manual typewriters, a surveillance society operating with wire-plug telephones. The viewer simply doesn't know where they are – or when. The semiotics is confusing, things look familiar but out of place.

The juxtaposition of future dystopia and wartime nostalgia makes it difficult for the viewer to settle into ready-made assumptions about the world they are looking at. They can't distance it into a (*Casablanca*) past or a (*Blade Runner*) future. The film is about the ever present – the extraordinary madness that can, at any moment, erupt unannounced into an ordinary world. Like *Die Hard*, the enemy is 'terrorism', the difference is that it is far from 'foreign'.

The world of *Brazil* has created its own virtual reality – out of propaganda, plastic and pasteboard – which, for all the absurdity, more closely resembles the world *we* actually live in. The movie is an absurdist comedy that uses the blurring of genre to sharpen its satirical edge and the subversion of genre expectations to keep the audience guessing. This 'Brazil' is nowhere because it is everywhere – and now.

EXERCISE

Audience profile

Make a list of the generic features relevant to your film and the sorts of pleasure that derive from their inclusion.

Write out a detailed 'profile' of your target audience – their likes, dislikes and expectations, and the key texts within the genre that are likely to have informed their taste.

List the limitations that most sharply impinge on your film due to genre considerations. This should clarify the boundaries to the fictional 'reality' you must work within.

CASE STUDY

	Citizen Kane
	RKO Radio Pictures
Director	Orson Welles
Screenwriters	Herman J. Mankiewicz, Orson Welles
Cast including	Orson Welles (Charles Foster Kane)
	Joseph Cotton ((Jedediah Leland)
	Dorothy Comingore (Susan Alexander Kane)
	William Alland (Jerry Thompson)
Crew including	Gregg Toland (cinematography)
	Bert Shipman (camera operator)
	Robert Wise (editing)
	Van Nest Polglase (art director)
Tagline	The classic story of power and the press.

Synopsis

Charles Foster Kane dies. His immense public notoriety and colossal wealth make his death a media event. But the editor-in-chief of 'News on the March' is dissatisfied with the standard newsreel obituary and sends a reporter, Thompson, on a mission to discover the mystery behind Kane's last dying word: 'Rosebud'. Thompson interviews those who could claim to know Kane best, but the contradictory impressions he receives suggest an even greater enigma.

Intertexts

The movie begins with an array of striking images designed to implicate the viewer in the act of intruding upon a man's private life. The first thing to greet the audience is a visual joke, a 'No Trespassing' sign, beyond which the eye immediately wishes the camera to transgress.

This first scene may have been directly influenced by the famous opening of Hitchcock's *Rebecca* (1940) where the camera seems to pass magically through the iron gates of Manderley; another 'haunted' house. Whether or not this was an intentional reference, the movie's original audience is likely to have made the connection and expected a similar tale of romantic passion and murderous secrets.

In fact, *Citizen Kane* is completely free of such stock Hollywood material. What the two films do share is a retrospective narration orientated around the task of uncovering the truth behind the public image of the elusive central figure.

The sombre moment of Kane's death is shattered by the raucous signature music of a cinema newsreel reporting the event. It quotes the lines from Samuel Taylor Coleridge's famous poem, which gives the Kane estate its name: 'In Xanadu did Kubla Khan / A stately pleasure-dome decree'. Kane's legendary status and virtually limitless power and excess are instantly established by such exotic parallels.

The word Khan (or King) touches on the central ambiguity of Kane's political career. He begins as a democratic champion of the people, but gradually turns into a brutal despot – a contradiction the movie is about to explore.

The film bombards us with Kane's name and its biblical echoes are unavoidable. The story of Cain, the first son of Adam and Eve, and the murderer of his brother Abel – touches on themes that are deeply ingrained within the film, such as belonging and exile, brotherhood and selfishness. Kane suffers numerous childhood 'expulsions', exhibits massive egotism, and is ultimately cut off from worldly affection, lost and rootless in a desert land. In this case, the mark of 'Kane' is his notoriety – behind which he is a lonely isolated figure.

In addition to being a vast repository of European art, Xanadu is also 'the biggest private zoo since Noah'. This second biblical allusion suggests not just the desperation with which Kane has amassed everything he could lay his hands on ('the loot of the world'), but invites comparison between one man serving God and saving His Creation, and another feeding his ego by creating a world of his own.

The fictional screen obituary hosts a wealth of appropriated material including operatic recordings and stock newsreel footage. These 'real' documentary images are mixed with 'faked' ones, which appear to show Kane rubbing shoulders with Hitler. In 1941, the technology did not exist to produce the effects we see in *Zelig*, (in fact, Woody Allen's film is alluding in part to this moment in *Citizen Kane),* but Welles nevertheless created a curious effect for a cinema audience that only minutes before had been watching a 'real' newsreel probably alluding to the very same political figures.

Genre > **Case study: Citizen Kane**

Urtext

Two immensely compelling stories underlie *Citizen Kane – Achilles* and *Orpheus*. Kane is a larger-than-life tragic hero with a fatal flaw. Everyone Thompson speaks to seems to concur with this, but there is no consensus as to what this critical defect actually was. The most thorough account of 'Charlie' seems to come from his oldest friend, Jedediah Leland, who tells us that he simply wanted everyone to love him unconditionally.

True or not, and no one interpretation of Kane seems adequate, we are certainly pointed in the direction of a man trying to recapture what he lost in childhood. Some in the film speculate it was 'Rosebud'. But in the attempt to find it he was distracted by power and 'things' (and at one point a woman's laughter). The film also sends us on that journey.

**Citizen Kane
(dir: Orson Welles 1941)**

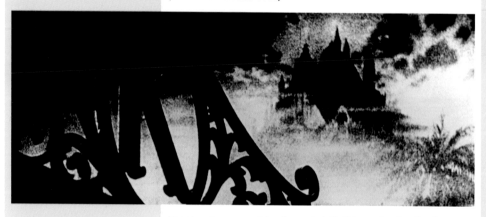

Kane's refuge resembles those dark Gothic castles familiar from tales by Bram Stoker and Edgar Allan Poe. There is certainly something vampiric in Kane's relationships with other people, and the house itself is a grotesque mausoleum where he has chosen to bury himself and his wife *alive*.

Meta-discourse

Citizen Kane is highly self-reflexive; drawing attention to the language of film. The news documentary enlists a whole repertoire of associated journalistic discourses: the loud-hailer voice-over, political speeches, personal interviews, library pictures, spy footage, official records, illustrative maps, spinning newspaper headlines. The narration adopts a variety of modes and tones: informative, triumphant, dramatic, revelatory, mythic, historical, topical, scandalous, comic, elegiac.

More than mere imitation, the dazzling variety and sheer energy of the mock report sums up the media world of which Kane is both a promoter *and* a product. Welles' performance makes Kane as mercurial and ephemeral as a copy of his beloved *Inquirer* – his identity is a thing he is constantly 'making up' as he goes along, creating an artificial reality to suit himself. In more ways than one Kane is a media creation.

The moment that the newsreel ends is truly startling. As the piece of film we have been watching suddenly becomes a 'text' – an artefact under construction, so too does the entire movie into which it is embedded. The whole materiality of cinema is compressed into the sound of a reel running out, a beam of white light cutting across the darkness, and an editor calling up to a projection room. Suddenly, the raw condition of all film is made present to us, just as it was for Welles and his team when they first sat and viewed the film's rushes at a screening exactly like this.

Citizen Kane playfully breaks the unwritten rule against revealing its own artifice, but in so doing it cements a different relationship with a cinematically literate audience that can enjoy being taken into a film-maker's confidence to explore the mechanisms that make film work. One of these is genre.

Glossary

Urtext: An original or the earliest version of a text, to which later versions can be compared.

Glossary:

Film noir: A largely American film genre often based around crime fiction. Has its roots in German expressionism.

Genre

Aesthetically, Welles and his cinematographer adopt the visual idiom of **film noir** – extremes of light and deep shadow, exaggerated angles, distortions of scale, and an extended depth of visual field. Because it is associated with gritty crime dramas of dark underworld dealings and even darker motives, this stylisation encourages the audience to suspend its judgement and look beyond the surface appearance of things, towards some deeper mystery.

Citizen Kane may not be a 'whodunnit', but it *is* a 'who-was-he' – a detective investigation attempting, through a splintered structure of interlocking flashbacks, to piece together the man behind the name.

Much of the controversy that surrounded the film on its first release related to the fact that it appeared to be a thinly veiled portrait – a biopic – of a real-life tycoon and media magnate, William Randolph Hearst. But the movie has a very complex and extensive intertextual relationship with American politics in general, which goes well beyond one individual.

The representation of Corporate America on the one hand and the mechanics of popular democracy on the other constitute a serious discourse that Welles was clearly interested to explore. The fact that Kane can be characterised as a communist one moment and a fascist the next makes him a telling comment on a political culture in which the absence of any real principles may be a positive electoral advantage. Kane (as the name might suggest) is a hollow man.

Innovation

Citizen Kane is the most celebrated movie in Hollywood history. If innovation and originality exists anywhere it is here. And yet, even in this unconventional and technically groundbreaking film, we can see the auteur figure of Orson Welles calling upon the ready-made intertextual resources at his disposal. Under his directorship, these 'other' materials may be reshaped, blended and even inverted, but without them the movie wouldn't have come into being. Welles' genius was in knowing what to do with them – knowing how to bend them to his particular purpose.

Intertextuality

**Citizen Kane
(dir: Orson Welles 1941)**

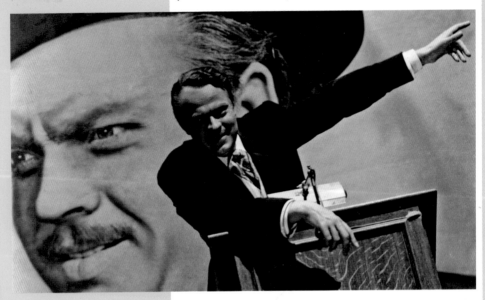

One final intertext is the life and career of Welles himself. Kane's hostility to the established order and his determination to attack it from the inside mirrors something of Welles' own position within the Hollywood studio system. Regrettably, Welles never again had the creative freedom to bite the hand that fed him.

DISCUSSION QUESTIONS

Citizen Kane abounds with signifiers that relate to other films and other films are full of references that relate back to it. When watching other works that relate to this iconic example consider why they are making these references; what does it do or say to an audience?

Citizen Kane borrows from the techniques of film noir. Why is this so? Do we find comfort in genre?

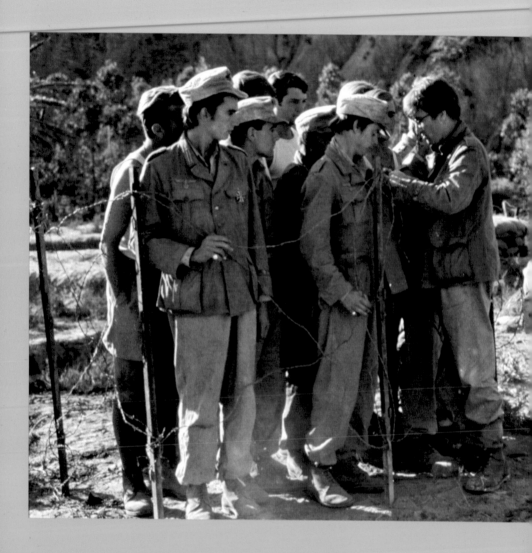

IDEOLOGY

**How I Won the War
(dir: Richard Lester 1967)**

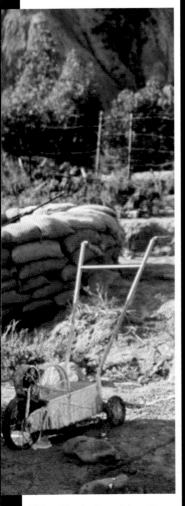

Richard Lester is an interesting director for those who are intrigued by the disruption of reality and film form. His playful style reminds the audience that they are watching a piece of fiction. The inclusion of John Lennon is no accident; it offers a very late-1960s attitude to an early-1940s setting.

Ideology is a difficult and slippery term. There are many, many books that seek to explain ideology and they all seem to arrive at different definitions. This is not to suggest it is a term that has no use, nor does it have multiple uses; rather it has specific uses. The consideration of ideology is essential in cinema whether you are a film-maker, a theorist, a critic or simply a member of an audience.

Ideology is pervasive. As with narrative and semiotics, ideology is part of human communication and stretches to every part of life. However, film communicates in a specific way and as such transmits ideology in a particular way and this is what we need to consider.

Ideological analysis

The uses of ideological analysis for the theorist or the critic are pretty self-evident. The function of the study of ideology for the film-maker is similarly clear. The most dangerous position a film-maker can take is to think that they are free of ideology. We all have our beliefs, our views, and our social and cultural positions. Some of these are known to us, others are so deeply embedded that they appear to be 'natural'.

So what is ideology?

Ideology is difficult to pin down and, given that it is everywhere, it is difficult to isolate. However, cinema is a specific medium, and, as has been discussed, it uses its own codes and conventions. Therefore the ideological aspects of cinema can be examined in order to understand its specific impact and why it is so powerful.

When you watch a film you are engaging in the transmission of knowledge. When you make a film you are communicating something to an audience – whether you mean to or not. That is one of the issues with ideology; it is unseen. For example, think of your own behaviour when you attend the cinema: do you attend as a student of cinema or even as a film-maker, or do you go to be entertained? Ideology is at its most invidious and powerful when its audience is relaxed, receptive and unaware that they are exposed to it.

Despite earlier comments that ideology is essentially impossible to define, without some working definition any further discussion would be equally impossible. In defining ideology the complexities of the term are drawn out.

Text and context

Over time two broad schools of thought have developed around the nature of ideology and how cinema should be treated – these can be defined as text and context. Text looks at film as film, and draws out of it themes that reflect back on society while context looks at the context in which the film was produced.

Real analysis comes at the intersection of these two views. For the film-maker this is a difficult position to adopt. After all, it means trying to establish your film's ideological impact before you have even made it. In terms of text, this requires being aware of the specific language(s) you use and the controls you place on the film's form. Context is harder; this relies on you having absolute control, or at least minimising the control others have. It is also requires you to be wholly aware of your own position as an individual to clearly see how your own ideological viewpoint fundamentally impacts on the shape and nature of your film.

Time and place

It seems an obvious statement to note that what you believe is hugely dependent on where you come from and when you live. Theories of ideology suggest that as complex individuals we are actually an amalgam of the specific experiences that have gone to 'construct us'. This means that there might be universal ideologies that we share, but there are also specific issues that are contingent to time. This is sometimes referred to as 'contextual determinism'. This idea is best exemplified by watching any science-fiction film, which date at a faster rate than any other genre.

Defining ideology

Ideology is a systematic body of ideas, attitudes, values and perceptions. It is also the collective views, attitudes, positions and dogmas of a societal group. Ideology is both specific and general. It is seen and unseen. It can be conscious, but is more often unconscious. It is pervasive and impacts on every aspect of human existence.

Collective authorship

While film directors often like to believe that they are the 'auteur', single-handedly dictating every aspect of their film's development, there are countless people who influence what appears on screen. The production of a film is a collective process in part, but a hierarchical one in others. This hierarchy and the nature of collaboration shifts in relation to the stage of production you are in.

The structuralist approaches outlined in Chapters 1 and 2 suggest that meaning is generated between the flickering images on the screen and the individual sitting in the audience. However, although the film-maker sets the parameters of meaning (they decide what appears on screen) this is actually affected by a great number of things and the input of a large number of people. The many variables that affect what appears on screen can render statements about what a director (or editor or composer, and so on) 'meant' largely irrelevant. The idea that an audience 'reads meaning into a film' is quite right; actually this is the analysis of what appears on screen by the audience. This also means that the circumstances on the day of filming might subtly but importantly change what things mean in the *mise en scène*. Pinpointing the original ideological impetus becomes increasingly difficult, and in fact there may be an ideology or ideologies present that you never intended to put there.

Examine the simplified view of the production flow for a film shown opposite in terms of who takes responsibility where. There are many people who are vital to the production of the film, and many who have a profound impact on the aesthetic and thus the form of the film. It is these people who are crucially shaping the ideological world view the film presents and represents.

EXERCISE

Analysing propaganda
View a classic of propaganda, such as Leni Riefenstahl's *Triumph of the Will* (1934). Do you find it difficult to see why people were taken in by something so blatant? If so, imagine yourself in Weimar Germany in 1936 with no knowledge of the atrocities the Nazis were perpetrating – now how does the film look? Such is the power and danger of film.

Production flow

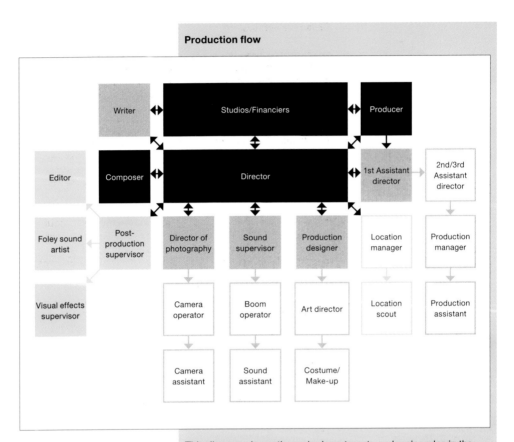

Key

Blue outline	pre-production
Blue box	post-production
Grey outline	production
Grey box	pre-production and production

This diagram shows the main departments and major roles in the production process. Most feature films have personnel lists running into hundreds of people; short films can be as few as five or six with people doubling up on roles.

The composer stands outside the main production process and is commissioned at the start of the process and then again at the end. The omni-present figures are the director, the producer and, of course, the studios/financiers.

Form

While it is undoubtedly true that the way in which characters behave and what they say is partly how film ideology is communicated, this is simply one level of meaning. There is much more complexity to it than that. This is where the notion of film form comes into play.

A film's form often goes unnoticed by its audience, and this is what makes it so essential to its ideological impact. In fact, most viewers suspend their disbelief when they enter the cinema. Earlier chapters have demonstrated the specific codes and conventions that film uses. If the audience focuses on these codes and conventions, rather than the story or experience they are conveying, the film would make little sense. It might even seem absurd. Therefore the form a film takes has to remain hidden to its audience, while being wholly visible to the film-maker.

Let's take a look at *Dirty Harry* as an example. While there is still an undoubted cool to Clint Eastwood's Harry Callaghan character, it is now very easy to mock the flares and feel very distant from the message. This is to miss the point of the ideological impact the film is having on us. Look at the form of the film. While Harry is certainly morally questionable, the 'bad guys' are worse and he always gets results. Harry is presented as the only chance of bringing salvation to the sympathetic characters in the film, and the viewer wants him to win. Outside the context of this film, this may potentially perpetuate a fairly right-wing view of individualism and the right to violence.

My movie is born first in my head, dies on paper; is resuscitated by the living persons and real objects I use, which are killed on film, but placed in a certain order and projected on to a screen, come to life again like flowers in water.

Robert Bresson, director

**Dirty Harry
(dir: Don Siegel 1971)**

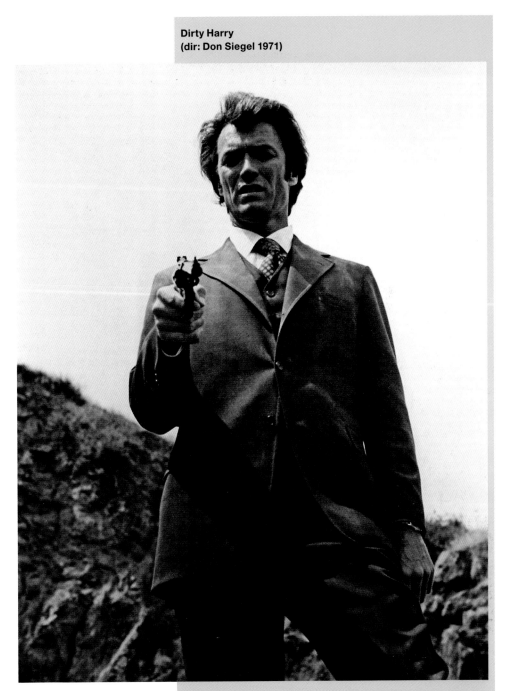

Dirty Harry is a classic example of a film that bears the hallmarks of 1970s attitudes to violence, gender and race.

As with ideology, there are many definitions for 'realism'. A good starting point is to think of realism as an amalgam of the devices used by film-makers to disguise the fact that what the viewer is shown isn't real. In other words, realism is the illusion that what is shown on-screen is in some way connected to reality. Of course, what's on-screen is not reality; just because it is recognisable it doesn't mean that it is real. It's still just flickering lights in a dark room – where meaning is generated between audience and screen.

Historical context

The term 'realism' emerged in mid-19th-century France to refer to a particular kind of fine art. A key factor in its development was the camera and particularly the public reception of photographs. The belief was that the camera was able to capture an objective truth about the world. The illusion must have been powerful, as this view spread to the other arts. As cinema became established, it is no accident that realism quickly became a dominant form of expression. Film-makers in the 19th and 20th centuries believed that they could present a truth about the world through fiction, again as if they were not part of it and were placing no bias upon it.

The theorists

There are many theorists who have dissected the concept of realism and its dominance. The three who stand out more than any others, and who have lent their ideas to decades of later theorists, are Rudolf Arnheim (1904–2007), André Bazin (1918–1958) and Siegfried Kracauer (1889–1966). Of the three, it is Bazin who remains most influential in his view of cinema's ability to record and represent reality. As he noted: 'photography does not create eternity, as art does; it embalms time, rescuing it simply from its proper corruption'. By which he implies that it also has a historical purpose in capturing a view of the world forever. However, this is problematic because, unlike real life, film usually presents a clear viewpoint; it offers ideological resolution, if not narrative resolution. Thus realism inevitably presents ideological unity, and an ideological world view.

How realism works

Realist film presents what appears on the screen as natural. A key means of achieving this is to make it appear unmediated and this is often achieved through the narrative as much as it is through the form. It is this that allows realism to take so many forms. For example, many non-realist films ensure that the hero is clearly identifiable, but this would simply not work in a realist film. To make a protagonist appear as a real person, rather than a 'real film character' they need to embody characteristics that the audience will perceive as being close to their understanding of reality. This often includes moral ambiguity of some kind. And, as with real life, conclusions are not always neat in realist films, or they appear not to be neat even when there is a resolution within the filmic narrative. It is a film's ability to tell the viewer what to think, balanced with an illusion of free choice, which makes it so powerful. There are many realist films that are well worth examining, amongst the most notable are Jean Renoir's *Toni* (1935) and Sidney Lumet's *The Hill* (1965).

EXERCISE

Reading personal ideology
Select a photograph that is familiar to you and show it to two or three of your friends. Ask them to describe what they see and the context they imagine the photograph was taken in. Then ask them to identify the signifiers that are providing this information.
You may find that they have created a narrative about what they see.

Repeat the exercise with a cropped film still. Take out sections of the *mise en scène*. When they believe the film still is a photograph do your friends invest it with some authority – do they trust what they see? How does this change when they know it is fiction?

Recommended viewing

It is a useful exercise to view a film such as *La Règle du Jeu* (dir: Jean Renoir 1939) and compare it to a film such as *My Name is Joe* (dir: Ken Loach 1998). These are radically different films, but share many aspects of form.

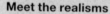

Meet the realisms

To complicate matters there are multiple forms of realism available to see and to use and they cover a variety of genres and forms. The various forms may seem fairly disparate, yet they are connected in their attempt to present unity, totality and a connection to the real world. The following list covers some of the most common forms of realism:

- **Magic realism:** where elements that might be associated with the fantastic intrude into film form. This may be subtle, as with *The Night of the Hunter* (dir: Charles Laughton 1955) or overt as in *Pan's Labyrinth* (dir: Guillermo del Toro 2006). In both cases, the use of fantastic elements emphasises and/or underscores the realism of the main theme. Not to be confused with fantasy film.

- **Dirty realism:** where stories are reduced to the barest elements. This often leads to a bleak quality. Established as a literary movement in America, this has spread to cinema, particularly in the UK with films such as *Red Road* (dir: Andrea Arnold 2006).

- **Gritty realism:** a critical term assigned to a number of films that tend towards the bleak but also try to capture the nature of everyday life. This extends to the work of people such as Ken Loach, but also to films like *28 Days Later* (dir: Danny Boyle 2002).

- **Heroic realism:** this incorporates the cinema of the Nazi regime and Soviet Russia. This includes films that support the dominant political viewpoint and is often aligned to propaganda.

- **Naturalism:** a movement that seeks to locate the individual at the centre of the story, and to show them as a victim of natural forces. It involves close attention to detail in the *mise en scène* to make film form look 'natural', as in the work of Jean Renoir.

Social realism

Social realism is a form of filmic expression that prioritises depictions of working-class life and portrays this lived experience as legitimate. Three key examples are:

- **Soviet socialist realism:** a form of realism dictated by the state during the establishment of the Soviet state. This was an important movement in that it was the first to fully recognise the ideological potential of cinema and other artistic forms. The works of Soviet socialist realism simply support the dominant political view, often by unusual forms. The most notable film-maker to work within this form was Sergei Eisenstein.

- **Italian neo-realism:** as a form for production, neo-realism is interesting as it was developed by critics writing for a film journal. It is no accident that the movement emerged during Mussolini's stranglehold on Italy. In these terms, it emphasised democracy and the proletariat. The main focus was on lived experience, the emotions of 'real people'. To preserve the illusion of reality many films used 'real' people rather than actors. Locations that stressed the desolation caused by the Second World War brought the message of the films closer to the audience. Formally, there is a lack of lighting and complex sound dubbing. The first work of neo-realism is often seen as *Rome, Open City* (dir: Roberto Rossellini 1945). Other key practitioners include Vittorio de Sica, Federico Fellini and Michelangelo Antonioni.

- **Kitchen sink realism:** this movement emerged during the 1950s in Britain and stems from a tradition of social concern stemming from Charles Dickens. The form has developed alongside the gradual decline of Britain as an industrial power and is set in Northern England. A key characteristic is the use of dialect, accent and real locations. Early works such as *Look Back in Anger* (dir: Tony Richardson 1958) show the clash of the modern against tradition with youth being a key feature. Important directors such as Lindsay Anderson and Ken Loach stemmed from this period. The movement developed and continues to inform British cinema to this day with directors such as Mike Leigh, Mark Herman and Shane Meadows.

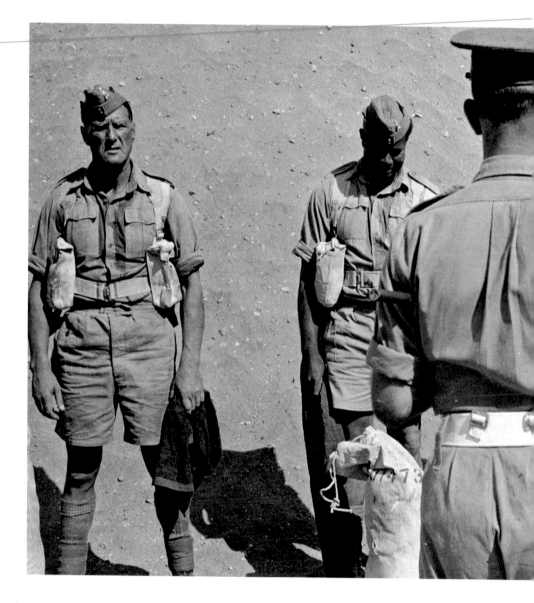

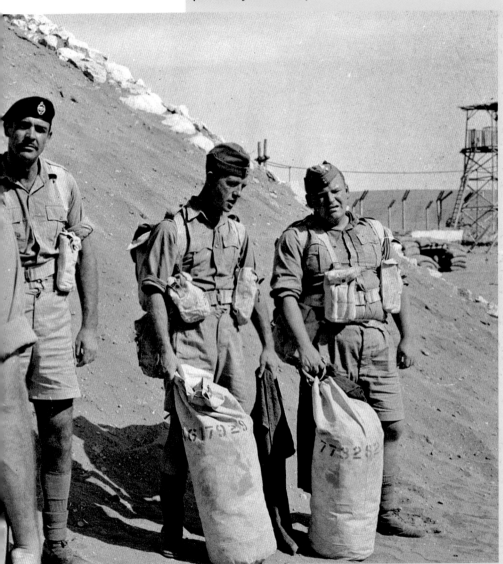

**The Hill
(dir: Sidney Lumet 1965)**

The Hill presents us with what appears to be morally ambiguous characters. We never know whether Joe Roberts is guilty or not, yet it is impossible not to take his side. Beyond characterisation the skill and power of the film is in the form. Set in an internment camp, there is the omnipresent sound of marching boots and no music at all. This locates the audience in the camp and makes them feel the pressure and pain of the lead characters.

Ideological analysis > **Realism** > Ideology and genre

Dogme 95

An interesting case study of more contemporary attempts to develop a realist movement is Dogme 95. This was a short-lived movement established in Denmark in 1995 by Lars Von Trier and Thomas Vinterberg.

One facet unique to the group was that they set out their aims in a manifesto, which they referred to as a 'vow of chastity'. This was a clear move back to the principles established by the neo-realists. However, unlike this earlier movement, Dogme was focused on form rather than the fundamental relationship between form and content.

**Festen
(dir: Thomas Vinterberg 1998)**

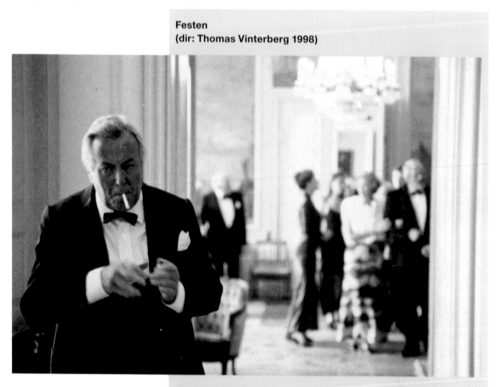

Festen is a fiction film based on a true story. It is a fascinating film and exists in part as an experiment with the Dogme style. Professional actors and crew work with the techniques to create an unsettling effect, which matches the subject in hand. It is interesting to note that most of the Dogme films continue with bleak themes.

The Dogme 95 vow of chastity

I swear to submit to the following set of rules drawn up and confirmed by Dogme 95:

1 Shooting must be done on location. Props and sets must not be brought in (if a particular prop is necessary for the story, a location must be chosen where this prop is to be found).

2 The sound must never be produced apart from the images or vice versa. (Music must not be used unless it occurs where the scene is being shot.)

3 The camera must be hand-held. Any movement or immobility attainable in the hand is permitted. (The film must not take place where the camera is standing; shooting must take place where the film takes place.)

4 The film must be in colour. Special lighting is not acceptable. (If there is too little light for exposure the scene must be cut or a single lamp be attached to the camera.)

5 Optical work and filters are forbidden.

6 The film must not contain superficial action. (Murders, weapons, etc must not occur.)

7 Temporal and geographical alienation are forbidden. (That is to say that the film takes place here and now.)

8 Genre movies are not acceptable.

9 The film format must be Academy 35mm.

10 The director must not be credited.

Furthermore I swear as a director to refrain from personal taste! I am no longer an artist. I swear to refrain from creating a 'work', as I regard the instant as more important than the whole. My supreme goal is to force the truth out of my characters and settings. I swear to do so by all the means available and at the cost of any good taste and any aesthetic considerations.

Thus I make my VOW OF CHASTITY
Copenhagen, Monday 13 March 1995

On behalf of Dogme 95, Lars von Trier, Thomas Vinterberg

Ideological analysis > **Realism** > Ideology and genre

Every film connects to a genre in some form or another; no film is separate from either genre or movement. Genre is important for many reasons, not just for the audience, but also for the film-maker and studio. The relationship between genre and ideology is a fundamental one and yet it is easy to overlook.

What is genre?

In essence, genre is a signifying practice that has emerged over time by the repeated use of particular codes and conventions. Genres may stem from literary sources through adaptation or be specific to film. They are used by audiences in selecting a film, as the genre often gives an indication of a film's style and content. In this way, they can be used by the film-maker to either meet or subvert audience expectations. Studios like genres as they provide a useful marketing tool and have established measures of success.

Genre's relationship to ideology

Genre plays a fundamental role in setting the ideological framework of a film. On one level an audience is so familiar with the codes a genre piece employs that it works in the same way as realism – it lulls an audience into a false sense of security and thus a message can pass quickly and easily from film-maker to viewer. There are certain pre-existing ideological principles that exist within genres that revisionist or hybrid genres can use or challenge, as long as they are there in some form. In film noir, this would include gender positions where the hero is male and morally ambiguous and the female characters are either the *femme fatale* or the perfect damsel in distress.

Unravelling ideology

While there are semioticians and narratologists who specialise in film, there are very few film specialists in the world of ideological studies. It can therefore be useful to return for a moment to the origins and main points of the analysis of ideology outside of film studies.

Many of the thinkers involved are Marxists but 'Marxist' criticism shouldn't be conflated with political belief; although many of the concepts are shared, the emphasis is very different. Some of the key terms are explained in the boxes opposite.

Marxism

Base and superstructure: In traditional Marxist terminology 'base' refers to finance – the economic base of society. The 'superstructure' is the socio-cultural world that surrounds the economic base. This suggests that as film is a medium reliant on money it will always be controlled by the base. In Marxist terms this is true of all forms, but it is particularly evident in cinema.

Dialectic: According to Karl Marx the term 'dialectic' refers to two opposing forces that, through conflict, reach a resolution. As the essence of drama is conflict, this plays a fundamental role in film form. However, as a simplified form (film only normally lasts for about two hours or so), the nature of conflict has to be simplified.

Structuralist Marxists

Hegemony: Antonio Gramsci states that hegemony is leadership or dominance, usually of one social group over another. In terms of cinematic ideology, this can be seen in the systems that a film will use to make its ideology appear natural. In cinema this would be the repeated and often subtle prioritisation of one viewpoint over another.

Post-structural Marxists

Interpellation: According to Louis Althusser interpellation is where the individual already exists as a subject receptive to ideology. In these terms, this is where film plays to our existing expectations about who and what we are. Normally this is the notion of individuality as outlined by the 'hero'.

CASE STUDY

	Without Wires Batmen Productions/Sun Entertainment/York St John University
Director/ Screenwriter	Alex Woodcock
Producer	Saara Malmioja
Cast including	Michael Murray (Joseph Marland) Claire Devlin (Gemma Sharp-Harker)
Crew including:	Chris Downes (cinematography) Chris Snelling (editing) Cherie Bryant (production design) Tom Cockram/Tom Keith (sound)
Tagline	Lost innocence inside and outside the battlefield.

Without Wires: Time, place and character

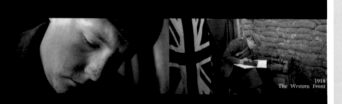

Without Wires firmly locates the protagonist, Joseph Marland, as a pensive and thoughtful figure and the location in the trench clearly shows setting in time and place.

The inclusion of the Union Jack is a clear symbol of nationality, but also carries notions of the jingoism that characterised the First World War.

Ideology

Synopsis

Take a look at the short film *Without Wires* (2008) – available at www.avabooks.ch/index.php/ava/bookdetails/978-2-940411-27-6. A weak, war-weary sun rises up over the churned and pitted fields of the Western Front. But the sun isn't rising in silence, the thunder and lightning of a barrage of artillery accompanies its ascendance. The natural wonder of darkness being chased away and the man-made carnage of warfare do battle for a man's attention. But his mind is no longer reachable; it is far away in distance and time, back in the hallowed halls of English academia, four years ago.

The heady smell of learning from the musty books is joined by the delicate lavender scent a young lady wears, standing at a bookshelf amongst the rows and rows of weighty tomes. Her strong independence and his unerring gentlemanly ways are about to intertwine over a single volume.

Back in his trench, long since separated from the main battle group, with no superior officers to guide him and a handful of junior soldiers looking to him for orders, guidance and most of all hope, his narrowing odds of survival are no match for his passion for the past. His shortening future carries no significance. Did the decisions he made years ago lead him to this place and time, or did he fall foul of the fates that would have brought him here regardless?

Ideology and the short film

There is very little to differentiate short films from feature films in terms of their ability to communicate ideology. However, the way in which they communicate ideology is down to the specifics of the form and this is dictated by the differential in semiotic communication and narrative construction. One crucial distinction to bear in mind is the context of viewing. Audiences and their venues can never be fixed, and hopefully will be different across time, particularly with a successful film as it moves to larger festivals and finds improved distribution routes. It's worth remembering that the audience for short films is almost always different from the audience of feature films; different in terms of what they expect. As an analyst, you cannot second guess what the film-maker 'meant' and as a maker you cannot hope to capture all the audience in your planning. However, you can bear this factor in mind.

Without Wires started life as a student film, but broke with all the clichés regarding scope, scale and ambition. Small aspects of the form, such as the 16:9 presentation, the end credits and the depth of field scream 'movie'. The additional marketing and festival submission make this a film that stands out from the usual.

Without Wires: Authenticity

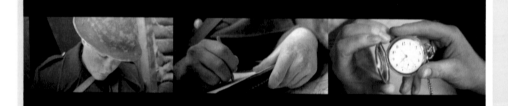

The evident squalor of the trench confirms the accuracy of the film in its portrayal of the First World War, or rather it appears to be authentic and as such exists as a realist film. The fact that Marland is writing and looking at the watch suggests death is imminent without spelling it out.

Without Wires/with realism: The form

Without Wires is a realist film. This seems an odd statement when it is a First World War drama. Surely the historical setting should take it away from our perspective of what constitutes reality? But, of course, Realism is nothing to do with reality at all. As we've already seen, it is the devices a film uses to make us believe that what is being shown is real. *Without Wires* uses the conventions of the realist historical drama that have emerged post *Barry Lyndon* (dir: Stanley Kubrick 1975). This includes providing the audience with a veneer of historical fact, which hides the contemporary story lines within. *Without Wires* uses carefully selected locations and costumes tied to the story and the difficult-to-film trench locations are shot in close-up (which also matches the importance of the protagonist's emotion).

Ideology and history

Without Wires uses dialogue that to modern ears might appear archaic. As it sounds like it could come from 1914, and as we have little access to speech patterns from 1914, it is our only reference. Therefore, it is real. The other subtle factor that furthers the realism inherent in the film is dirt. Pre-1970s Westerns tended towards clean heroes and attractive homesteads. When Clint Eastwood directed *High Plains Drifter* (1973) the settings became gritty and dirty and appeared more accurate – but who knows what it was really like in the 1860s in the Midwest of America? This is also true of furniture. If you look around your house you'll tend to see furniture from a number of historical periods. Early First World War dramas tended to make all their props and furniture appear to originate from around 1914. This had the inadvertent effect of moving the sets away from rather than closer to reality, or at least an audience's perception of reality. *Without Wires* works as everything looks old, but natural rather than simply 'period'.

This perception of accuracy is important to the process of ideological communication. It means that the audience is less likely to question the presentation and are subtly absorbed into the drama. The ideology can thus be communicated effectively.

Without Wires: The central relationship

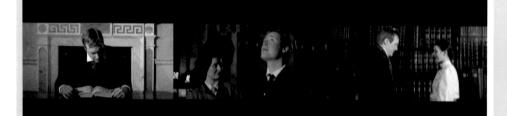

The interiors support the realism shown in the trenches.
The importance of the relationship between the two main
protagonists is emphasised by the absence of other people
in vast settings that would normally be filled.

Without Wires: Time runs out

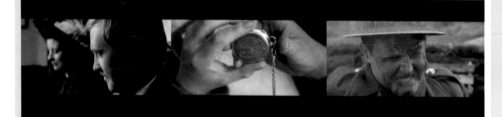

The intensity of the situation and the move to war is emphasised by
the use of close-ups on Marland. The message given by the return
to the watch is: the end has come, time has finally run out.

So what is Without Wires about?

It is impossible to be completely neutral in the analysis of any film as it is necessarily affected by the viewer's ideological position. However, there are certain narrative themes and signifiers in *Without Wires* that are worth exploring. On the surface, this is a story about the horror of war, any war, regardless of the First World War setting. However, there are other implicit messages which, as they are seemingly subsumed into the overarching war narrative, can manipulate us as an audience:

- **Class:** the film focuses on characters in the 'officer class' but also offers a glimpse of 'ordinary soldiers'. This suggests a debate on the contrast between the nature of leadership with and without peril.

- **Gender:** the female character, Devlin, is the stronger of the two protagonists. Despite the social restrictions of the film's setting, she is the radical. The comment on gender has a stronger impact exactly because she is rallying against the context in which she finds herself.

- **Individuality:** the film focuses on individuals. We spend time with Marland and see his horror, but his decision about whether or not to conform is driven by Devlin. This is not just because of her concern for him. It is also connected to her strong anti-war stance.

- **Nationalism/patriotism:** this comes from parental control, and in the drive for Marland to enlist. The result is clear at the end of the film.

Regarding authorship, some of the points above may have been intended, some of it may not be. As ideological beings we communicate, transmit and conform to ideologies all the time.

DISCUSSION QUESTIONS

Consider *Without Wires* among other examples of your choice. Can a film ever be an accurate representation of history?

What is the difference between ideology and propaganda? Is it merely intent?

Without Wires is set during the First World War, but what does it say about class and gender as ideological constructions? Does it manage to construct a view of class and gender?

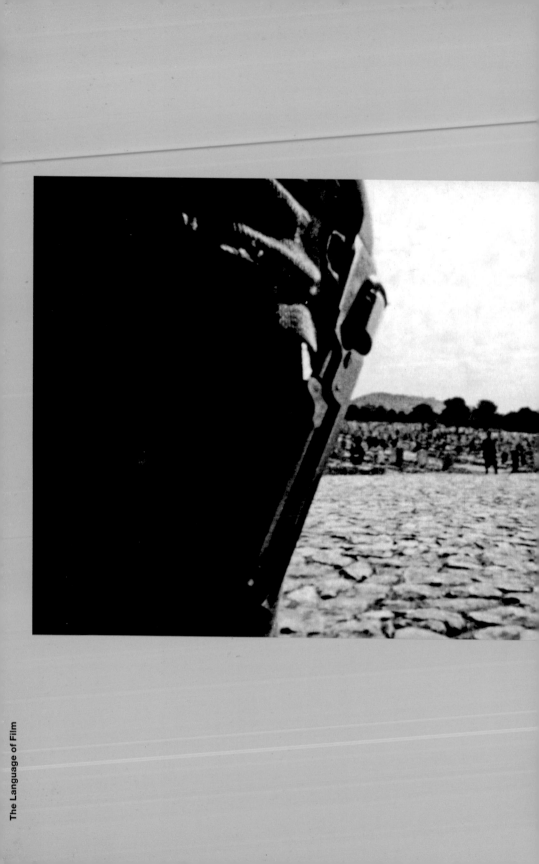

FRAMES AND IMAGES

The Good, the Bad and the Ugly (dir: Sergio Leone 1966)

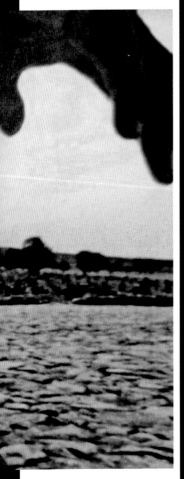

With very few exceptions, every film is made up of hundreds of different shots. Each one contributes a specific meaning to the film.

Everything within the frame of the image is selected for its meaning, from the colour of an actress's dress to the pattern on the wallpaper. In addition, the distance, height and angle of the camera all add meaning to the frame. We can never speak about the camera 'recording' what is in front of it. By its very action, the camera wrenches fragments of reality from their place in our world and translates them to celluloid or DV. It denatures, changes and adds meaning to what is before it.

The action staged in front of the camera is known as the pro-filmic event. This becomes cinematic only when we consider how the shot has changed the material. When we connect those images together in a sequence – the grammar of film, for want of a better term – further meaning is added, providing a context that adds meaning outside the image (we'll look at this in Chapter 6).

Film language has no distinctive grammar and its vocabulary is heavily reliant on context for its meaning. Every shot is chosen from an infinite number of possible framings, compositions and arrangements. When directors and cinematographers shoot, they draw on their experience with images for their targets.

Glossary

Abstract: To remove (like a dental abstraction) for scrutiny; a concern with form rather than content (as in abstract art).

The Soviet film-maker Sergei Eisenstein called the shot the basic unit of film. For him, a shot was a cell in a bigger organism, a construction he called 'montage'.

Perspective

The shot has its own vocabulary, one reliant on contexts of narrative and editing for meaning. Nevertheless, images can be read like words. Different shot angles, heights and types have their own established meanings derived from their use in thousands of films made over the last century or so.

The camera has several properties that transform and **abstract** the material depicted in front of the camera:

- Distance: The distance of the shot in relation to the actor or object being filmed.

- Height: The physical height of the camera in relation to the actor or object being filmed.

- Angle: The angle of the camera from the scene being filmed.

- Depth of field (focus): Sometimes the camera will only have shallow focus, with the background indistinct and out of focus (shot with a long lens) alternatively it can show everything in focus (deep focus with a short or wide-angle lens).

- Movement: Using a number of methods, from tilting the camera to moving it physically on tracks or a crane, moving the camera adds dramatic effect or simply avoids the need to cut.

Story and plot

Story and plot might seem the same but they are actually two different, but interrelated objects. According to David Bordwell and Kristin Thompson, the story is the linear sequence of events in the film while plot is the visual treatment of the story.

Story is composed of inferred events (things unseen but referred to in the story) and explicitly presented events.

Plot is composed of the same explicitly presented events and also added non-diegetic material (for example, the opening credits, sound, camera angles, editing and so on).

These two overlap and can't be broken apart – it is impossible to have a film story without those non-diegetic, narrational devices that present the story to the audience visually and structurally.

Whose eyes?

Every shot can be described in one of two ways: objective or subjective.

The majority of shots are objective. They show the viewer things in an 'impossible' way, giving them a godlike view of the events they are witnessing. Objectivity is about being detached and unobtrusive; documentary film-makers often attempt to be as objective as possible so as not to interfere with their subjects. Since someone has to choose where to put the camera, how to frame the shot and where to put the actors, objectivity is really an illusion. However, we still refer to these shots as objective.

Shots can also be subjective. Subjective shots show us the world from the perspective (the point of view or POV) of a character or object in the film.

In the opening scene of *Psycho* (1960), Alfred Hitchcock uses subjective shots from the point of view of the main character to portray her desire for power in her relationship with the married man with whom she is having an affair. The subjective shots depict her wish to become a subject with power, rather than just the 'other woman'. Hitchcock also uses POV shots from the perspective of a bundle of money, the true subject of the thriller. Atypically, he includes no subjective shots from the perspective of the man in this scene, who is weak willed and dominated by his father. Hitchcock here uses POV shots to give us a subtle sense of power in the scene, as well as to set up the narrative.

Recommended reading

Film Art: An Introduction (1979) by David Bordwell and Kristin Thompson is an in-depth and detailed analysis of film form and narrative systems. It provides the basis for some of the most used terminology in film studies.

> To me style is just the outside of content, and content the inside of style, like the outside and the inside of the human body. Both go together, they can't be separated.
>
> Jean-Luc Godard, film-maker

Glossary

Proscenium: A theatre stage or space that has a frame or arch as its main feature. Cinema still has very close links with theatre, and the camera frame was initially conceived as like a proscenium arch, as a window on the world. You will still see films shot in this style, such as Susan Stroman's stagey adaptation of *The Producers* (2005).

Diegesis: The fictional story world within the film, the sum of on-screen and off-screen space. Any object within the diegesis is diegetic, while anything in the film but not in its fictional world is non-diegetic (such as the score, credits and so on).

All shots have distance, height and level of some sort. For example, most shots of people are taken at eye level, but the camera's positioning can be manipulated for artistic or dramatic effect. Many shot types have long-established uses and meanings, although this is always bound to the context of the narrative. However, this does not always run according to rule and directors might exploit shots for the opposite or ironic effect.

Angles

Camera angle is normally split into three types:

- **Straight-on:** the camera is pointed straight at its subject. This can often be referred to as 'frontality'. Silent cinema was often frontal, with performers acting direct to camera, as though the audience was watching a theatre play in a **proscenium**.
- **Low angles:** the camera is positioned below the subject, looking up. Low angles can often suggest a powerful subject who looms over us.
- **High angles:** the camera position above the subject, looking down on them. High angles are often used to make the audience feel superior to whatever they are watching. Higher angles could also suggest voyeuristically intruding on a scene.

As mentioned above, directors do not always run true to form, and Orson Welles uses some of the lowest angles in *Citizen Kane* (1941), shot from a pit specially dug for the camera, at Kane's lowest point after an election defeat. Kane looms large over us, literally, although he is powerless.

The height of the camera works similarly. A low camera height can produce a low angle, although not necessarily. The Japanese director Yasujiro Ozu always shot characters at eye level no matter who he was shooting. The height was lower for children and babies. This often had the effect of making characters, unusually, speak directly into the camera during conversations. Although direct address by characters often reminds us we're watching a film, Ozu's style of shooting puts us right into the heart of the action.

On-screen/off-screen space

The camera can only depict what is in front of it; this is obviously on-screen space. Technically, the camera cannot present space to us because any 'space' in the image is an illusion of framing, lighting and the arrangement of actors and setting. We relate what we see on-screen to our understanding of our own reality to create a believable picture of the world on-screen, which we refer to as the diegetic space (the **diegesis**, the fictional story world).

In addition, renowned American film critic Noël Burch identified six zones of off-screen space:

- Left of the frame.
- Right of the frame.
- Top of the frame.
- Bottom of the frame.
- The back of the frame, usually filled with scenery or a location.
- The front of the frame, the 'fourth wall' which divides the diegetic space from the audience. Many film-makers choose to break this 'wall' by making characters address the audience directly to remind us we're watching a film rather than a 'slice of life'.

There are several ways in which off-screen space can be implied for the viewer:

- It can be spoken about in dialogue: characters can speak about other places the viewer can't see, this might be just across the road or a distant planet.
- A character or object can leave the frame, if we see a character leave frame right, we have to assume there is more space there: they can't just disappear!
- A character might glance at a character or an object outside the frame. Again, we have to assume something is there for them to look at.
- Just as characters can leave the frame, they can also re-enter, again implying a space beyond that which the viewer can see.
- On-screen sound is the most common method by which the audience is made to understand that there is a space beyond the camera's vision. Although it might have been added in post-production, it is diegetic sound emanating from a space within our story's world. Sound can suggest a 360° space (we'll look at this more in the next chapter).

Recommended viewing

Take a look at the opening of Francis Ford Coppola's *The Conversation* (1974); he chooses to begin with a long high-angle telephoto shot that scours a crowd for a couple talking about a murder. Think about how the height of the shot gives us a feeling of power, but also how sound is used to make us unsure of what we're looking for.

Recommended viewing

Watch the end sequence of
*The Good, the Bad and the
Ugly* (dir: Sergio Leone 1966)
and try to see how Leone uses
different shot distances to build
the tension toward a climax.
Also look at how he gives us a
view of the psychology of the
characters in close-up.

Shot distances are often dependent on the narrative,
genre and overall style of the film. Depending on the
context, shot types can have different meanings, although
an audience would still expect to see a close-up for an
important piece of dialogue or a character's reaction.
It is important to show significant details to make the
narrative work.

I'm ready for my close-up now

We can roughly identify each shot by their distance and the ways in
which they present setting and characters:

Extreme long shot (XLS): often used in Westerns or sci-fi films,
the XLS shows us massive backgrounds and tiny, often insignificant
people. Stanley Kubrick uses massive XLS in *2001: A Space Odyssey*
(1968) to show just how insignificant the human race is against the
infinite expanses of the universe.

Long shot (LS): human figures are more distinct, but background is
still very visible. Musicals, martial arts and action films often use lots
of long shots to let us see the action.

Medium long shot (MLS): the human figure is framed from around
the knees upwards. French critics refer to this shot as the *plan
américain* (American shot).

Medium close-up (MCU): individuals framed from the waist
upwards. This is one of the most typical shots in television, which,
due to its greater intimacy over the cinema screen, often avoids big
close-up shots.

Close-up (CU): generally emphasises individual details such as
faces, hands, feet, small objects. CUs are regularly used to give the
viewer an insight into significant narrative details: important character
reactions, a significant item (like a key being secretly hidden in
someone's pocket) or to stress the importance of a line of dialogue.

Extreme close-up (XCU): isolates very small details such as eyes,
lips, details of small objects. Sergio Leone loved to shoot XCUs of
eyes in his Westerns.

Camera level

The camera's level can also be changed to add additional meaning to the image. Canted, angled, images were popular in film noir to suggest the world losing control. After the Second World War, the US was rapidly changing, especially for men, and film noir portrayed this anxiety, often with unusual camera levels, dark lighting and moody, rain-slicked streets.

Of course, the reverse could also be true: the level of the camera might also be manipulated to make slanted objects appear flat. In *The Bed Sitting Room* (1969), Richard Lester shoots two characters attempting to drink from a can that pours upwards. Only when the scene cuts to a wider shot does the viewer understand that they are upside down. The initial shot portrays the absurdity of the situation and exposes the futile endeavours of the individuals trapped in this post-apocalyptic world.

Composition and power

The screen is generally assumed to be split into three portions. The middle of the screen is generally held to be the most powerful. If a character or object is framed centrally, they are given power over what is in the margins of the screen.

Again, the opposite is also true. In *Taxi Driver* (dir: Martin Scorsese 1976), the protagonist Travis is often framed in the margins of screen. This signals his own social marginality as a person on the edge. Sometimes Scorsese leaves Travis off-screen altogether to remind the viewer of his powerlessness, the very thing that leads to his shocking act of violence at the end of the film. All of the clues are visual, and added by camera style, rather than explained to us in **exposition**.

Glossary

Exposition: The means by which narrative information is relayed to viewers. This can be done visually, but is often conveyed in dialogue, an 'information dump' or a super-villain 'monologuing'.

EXERCISE

Combining shots
Select a five- to ten-minute sequence of any film. Try to break it down shot-by-shot. What types of shots does it use? What meanings do they contribute to what is depicted within the frame?

Distance, height and framing > Shot distances > Mise en scène

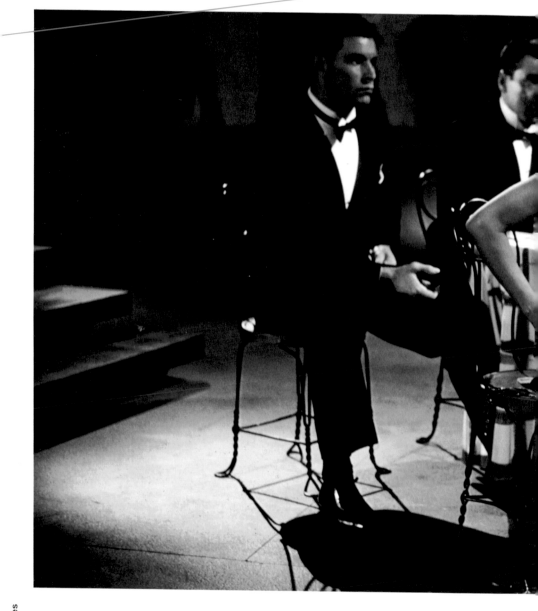

**Singin' in the Rain
(dir: Stanley Donen and Gene Kelly 1952)**

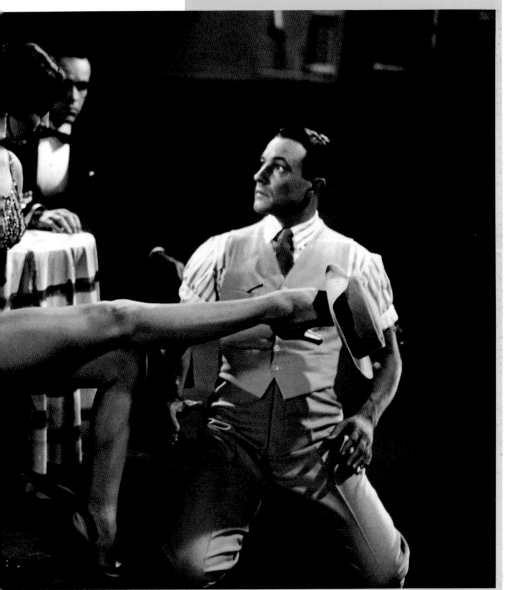

This long shot is typical of the musical, giving us a clear view of the dancers' movements, as well as the colourful background. Longer shots allow the film-maker to follow action without interruption, as well as letting us watch the bodies of dancers, one of the main pleasures of the musical.

Mise en scène is a critical term concerning the organisation of objects within the camera's frame. It does not include the angle and distance of the camera, although these provide a perspective to help the viewer's understanding of the material in the *mise en scène*. Additionally, it doesn't include things the viewer can't see, like sound.

**Without Wires
(dir: Alex Woodcock 2008)**

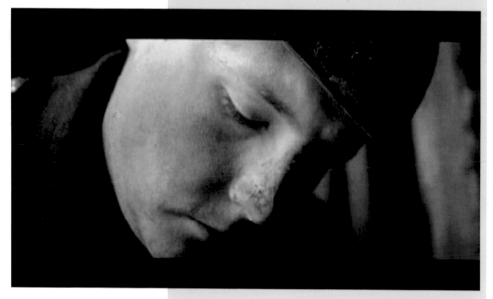

An example of a tight close-up. The viewer is allowed the opportunity to scrutinise the character's face without being able to see or understand the location. It's a very personal shot.

In the frame

Mise en scène is a French term derived from the theatre. Pronounced 'meez ahn sen', it literally means 'putting in the frame'. Everything we see within the camera's frame comes under the auspices of *mise en scène*: actors and their performances: lighting; costume; setting; coloured lens effects; theatrical blocking (the organisation of actors in space) and props. This all combines to give the viewer an image of cinematic space.

Lighting

Lighting is one of the most important elements of producing realistic or non-realist images. The most common lighting set-up is known as three-point lighting. It uses three lights to simulate a three-dimensional image.

- **The key light:** the brightest of the three, this highlights details on the face by casting shadow on the unlit portion.
- **The fill light:** usually positioned on the other side from the key, this light is softer and less bright, which lessens the effect of shadowing on the face.
- **The back light:** located behind the subject, the back light gives the subject the appearance of depth by creating a haloing effect around the subject. This means that the figure won't appear as a flat part of the background.

This is an important lighting technique that helps to create the illusion of a three-dimensional image. Remember that the film image is only a flat image projected onto a flat screen. Lighting is used to give the image the appearance of depth. Without this the viewer wouldn't perceive it as a 'real' image.

Lighting can be either high key or low key, depending on the emotional effect that the director and cinematographer are looking for. High-key (or high-contrast) lighting uses harsh light and black shadows to show a dark, dangerous and corrupt world. This is particularly popular in film noir. Low-key lighting is often used to manipulate mood. Horror films often use low-key lighting to hide monsters in shadows. In *The Day the Earth Stood Still* (dir: Robert Wise 1951) low-key lighting is used to suggest on-screen violence as our heroine is menaced just by the shadow of the massive robot Gort.

Tip

Keep in mind that once filmed, the actor is an object on-screen. They are surfaces composed of signs and symbols, and the viewer will tend to read them as such.

Shot distances > **Mise en scène** > The mobile camera frame

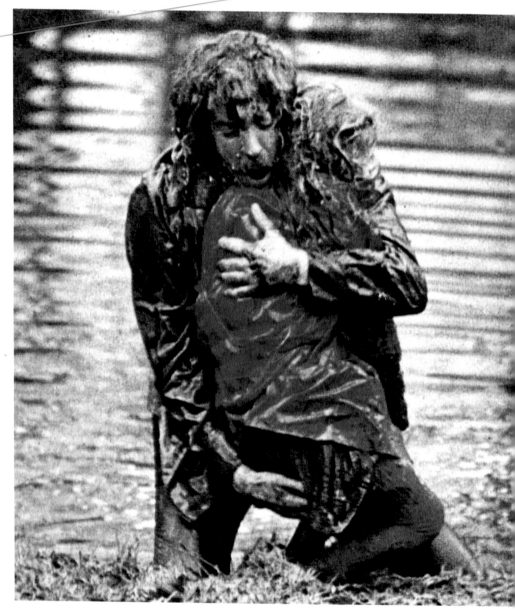

**Don't Look Now
(dir: Nicolas Roeg 1973)**

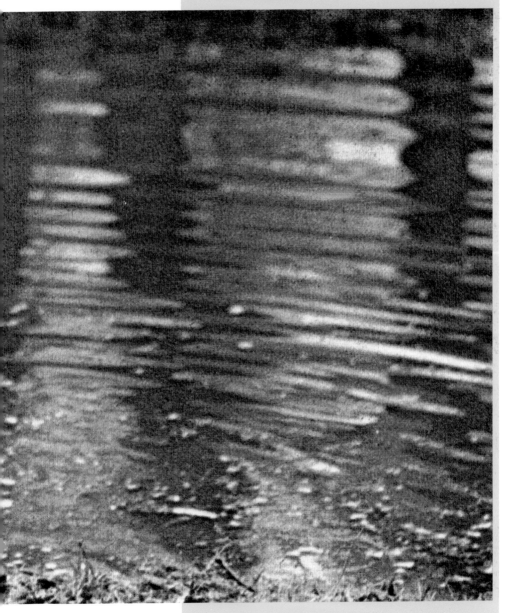

Throughout *Don't Look Now*, the bright red coat becomes a
repetitive motif in the *mise en scène*, symbolising John's guilt
around the death of his daughter, as well as playing a role in the
ghostly story of past and future.

Recommended viewing

Seek out *The Red Shoes* (dir: Michael Powell 1948) and watch its central ballet sequence. Think about its expressive use of colour, setting, costume and just about every other aspect of style in one of the most important visual sequences ever produced for the screen.

Expressionism

Expressionism is an important stylisation of *mise en scène*. Although the style has its roots in the early 20th century artistic movement in Germany and in the short-lived German expressionism movement, since then it has become an important tool of film-makers.

Expressionist films are overtly stylised. Realist films attempt to hide the marks of construction that remind the audience that they are watching a film. Expressionists, however, show the viewer all those things by overtly manipulating the image.

All elements of *mise en scène* can be manipulated to express the inner state of mind of a character or to express something about the film-maker. In *The Cabinet of Dr Caligari* (dir: Robert Wiene 1920), the setting is distorted and painted in jagged lines to express the mental turmoil of the protagonist. Similarly, the colour of Sister Ruth's lipstick in *Black Narcissus* (dir: Michael Powell 1947) is an intensified red to express her unbridled sexual libido.

This attention to detail can also be seen in this frame from *Eternal Sunshine of the Spotless Mind*, every aspect of which is meaningful. It is important to explore all elements of the *mise en scène*, as they have all been selected in order to provide meaning for us, whether it is telling us something about the character or about the story.

EXERCISES

Reading mise en scéne

Using the same sequence as the exercise on page 125, isolate a still frame and explore the individual signs of the composition and *mise en scène*. What does each element of *mise en scène* and framing say about the characters, their environment and the narrative?

Considering film style

Choose a film that you wouldn't normally watch, one that is outside your normal viewing experience. How might you describe the overall style of the film? What does it do differently?

**Eternal Sunshine of the Spotless Mind
(dir: Michel Gondry 2004)**

Since the majority of *Eternal Sunshine of the Spotless Mind* takes place in the mind of its protagonist, we can read many of the symbols in its *mise en scène* as expressionistic.

Shot: MCU framed just below eyeline. This shot gives us a clear view of Joel's face and the object he is scrutinising. Joel is framed slightly off centre – he is decentred, in emotional distress. He is not powerful at this point in the narrative, his life is out of control, and therefore Gondry does not frame him centrally.

Focus: The shot has a very shallow focus (probably digitally manipulated). This is an important clue to the narrative. Although we don't know it yet, we are inside Joel's head during the memory erasure procedure. His background is literally eroding. This is signalled for us visually.

Colour: Muted and dull, the colour again reminds us of the receding background.

Performance: Jim Carrey gives us a quizzical look. Joel is puzzled and perturbed, lost. How about the way he is holding the card? Does this look like a confident person in control? Does he hold the card like this just to remind us it's an important narrative object?

Costume: Although it seems obvious, Joel's hat and scarf remind us that it's cold.

The mobile camera frame

Recommended viewing

Take a look at a film that uses a subjective camera, such as *The Blair Witch Project* or *Cloverfield* (dir: Matt Reeves 2008), and think about how all of the properties of the camera, such as height, distance and the mobile frame are used to play around with the perspective of the camera, especially in their finales.

Recommended reading

Geoff King's *Spectacular Narratives: Hollywood in the Age of the Blockbuster* (2001) is an exploration of Hollywood cinema in the era of spectacles such as video games, theme parks and CGI. He in particular looks at how modern films are driven by a dynamic, often aggressive, style to shake the viewer.

Camera movement is one of the unique opportunities available to film over other art forms. In the early days of cinema, the camera was often static. It started to move during the silent era, but became static and theatrical when sound was introduced due to the bulky cameras. Since that time, cameras have become lighter and more manageable for camera operators to move, granting cinema an important dynamism and fluidity.

Panning, tilting and moving the camera

While camera movement can add speed and movement to the image, it can also counteract the need to edit a sequence together. The camera will reframe without cutting. A longer take might begin in close-up, move out to a wide shot and finish on a two-shot by reframing. This could be achieved by cutting, but by moving the camera, the director can suggest a much more unified and coherent sense of space within the frame of the camera, instead of constructing it afterwards through editing.

There are numerous ways in which the camera can move:

- **Pan (panorama):** the camera can pan left and right, as though turning its head on a horizontal plane.
- **Tilt:** the camera tilts up and down on a vertical line.
- **Tracking (dolly or trucking) shot:** the camera is fixed on a track, which can be laid in any direction.
- **Steadicam:** the camera is strapped to the camera operator using a special mount which produces smooth, floating shots that are more flexible than tracking shots. Stanley Kubrick used this to considerable effect in *The Shining* (1980) to suggest a fluid, disembodied presence following Danny's tricycle.
- **Hand-held:** similar to the Steadicam shot, but with a shaky effect that is often associated with a documentary-style realism or with the subjective POV of a character. The technique has also been used for horror films that claim to be composed of 'found footage', like *The Blair Witch Project* (dir: Daniel Myrick and Eduardo Sánchez 1999) or *Diary of the Dead* (dir: George A. Romero 2007).
- **Crane (also helicopter or airplane) shot:** mounting the camera to a crane can produce stunning shots from a great height, either to look down on diminished characters or to show scenery.

Simulated camera moves

Not all camera movement moves the camera; sometimes this can just be simulated:

- **Zoom:** a lens fitted to the camera allows the operator to change the focal length and alter the dimension of the image. For example, Robert Altman always shot with a telephoto lens to allow him to pick out significant detail in crowd scenes without letting his actors know. The speed of a zoom can also signify meaning, for example a fast zoom into the face of the villain in a martial arts film can be exciting, while a slow fade out from a character can be melancholic or sad.

- **Reverse zoom:** this is a special technique first used by Alfred Hitchcock in *Vertigo* (1958). It is achieved by tracking toward a character while simultaneously zooming out, changing focal length and making the background stretch into the distance. Hitchcock used it to suggest Scottie's vertigo, while Steven Spielberg uses the technique in *Jaws* (1975) to show Chief Brody's sudden realisation of another shark attack.

Camera movement

Camera movement is important in action films, where cuts can be made dynamic by jarring movement together. Normally a camera movement should be continuous across cuts, but directors can use jarring movement in opposite directions to produce impact and jar the viewer's senses. Geoff King has called these 'impact aesthetics'. They are used throughout *The Bourne Supremacy* (dir: Paul Greengrass 2004), especially where shaky hand-held close-ups are cut together jarringly.

Furthermore, because camera movement can suggest a much more realistic image of space, film-makers often use camera movement in conjunction with long takes to suggest a continuous space. For example, Jean-Luc Godard used very long hand-held tracking shots of Jean-Paul Belmondo and Jean Seberg in *Breathless* (1959) to create a unified sense of space, something he then disrupted with the use of jump cuts (we'll consider this in more detail in Chapter 6).

Logistically difficult but often stunning, the long take is one of cinema's most impressive features.

Duration

Not to be confused with long shots, the long take is a sequence of long duration. According to David Bordwell, the average shot length (ASL) in contemporary cinema is around 4–6 seconds, compared to 8–11 prior to 1960. A long take, however, could last up to around ten minutes – the length of a reel of film. In the era of digital video, this is becoming longer and longer; Alexander Sukurov's *Russian Ark* (2002) consists of just one shot spanning over 90 minutes and more than 200 years of Russian history.

The long take makes time in the image meet real time so that the diegetic time is the same as the discourse time (the time it takes to tell the story). Normally film-makers can contract or expand time to speed up events or to delay a climax; a good example is the 60-second countdown in *Star Trek II: The Wrath of Khan* (dir: Nicholas Meyer 1982), which takes more than two minutes!

André Bazin

André Bazin is probably the most significant film critic who ever lived. He co-founded the influential film journal *Les Cahiers du Cinéma* and helped promote the auteur theory, which stated that the director should be thought of as a film's author as they shape the visual treatment of the material. He also inspired many of the directors of the French Nouvelle Vague who wrote for *Cahiers*, many of whom, including François Truffaut, Jean-Luc Godard and Eric Rohmer, put Bazin's critical ideas onto the screen.

Bazin's most notable contribution was as a theorist of realism. He favoured long takes, shot in increased depth of field; whole sequences shot in single takes with every detail in focus. He claimed these 'sequence shots' were:

- More realistic – editing could only present reality a little more forcefully, creating false drama.

- More ambiguous – they allowed the viewer's eyes to wander, to pick out important information for themselves rather than have it made obvious via close-ups.

- More like looking at reality – Bazin thought anything that made the film image more like looking at real life was a good thing.

Frames and images

Time

Time can also be manipulated in several ways:

- Fast motion: the camera can run at slower than 24 frames per second (fps) to produce faster motion on playback; this is also known as 'under-cranking'.
- Slow motion: the camera is run at more than 24 fps to produce smooth slow motion, often up to around 2000 fps, which is becoming popular in sports broadcasting to scrutinise the action closely; also known as 'over-cranking'.
- Slow-motion effects can also be produced by duplicating individual frames; this produces a less fluid, jerkier slow motion.

Manipulating time in the image can be very effective. Slow motion can mythologise action, as in Sam Peckinpah's *The Wild Bunch* (1969), or emphasise simple moments, such as a close-up of two hands briefly touching in Hal Hartley's *Flirt* (1995).

Fast motion can often be used to make slow movements flow more realistically in 'real time': combined with long takes this can produce realist and spectacular effects. For example, Prachya Pinkaew includes a four-minute single-take sequence in *The Warrior King* (2005) that avoids cutting. This assures the viewer that no stunt doubles were used and the action was continuous, although it would have been filmed with slower action which is under-cranked. This realist effect reinforces the impact of the action for the audience.

Digital systems are now providing even more manipulations of time for impact. Take a look at how Zach Snyder compresses and expands time in *300* (2006) and *Watchmen* (2009) to emphasise the impact of violence, while the Wachowski brothers pioneered 'bullet time' in *The Matrix* (1999) to suggest the possibility of manipulating time in the computer-generated world of the matrix. Like the film-maker, the characters become able to manipulate time and space in their constructed world.

Recommended reading

André Bazin's most notable work is collected in *What is Cinema?* (1967). His article 'The Evolution of the Language of Cinema' argues for ambiguous reality over abstract editing, and is one of the most important critiques of film style ever written.

Recommended viewing

Watch the climactic gun battle in *The Wild Bunch* (dir: Sam Peckinpah 1969). Think about what the use of slow motion adds to the sequence: is this a celebration of violence? A mythology for the passing of the West? A bullet ballet?

Visual devices

The film-maker has a host of visual devices to narrate a story. Every shot is selected from an infinite number of unused options, each of which could bring a subtle or significant difference of meaning to a sequence.

The image is never simply produced to look interesting or entertaining, but to present a specific image of space, time and narrative meaning.

Cine-literacy is a matter of reading films, just as one reads a book by understanding its language and grammar. If you are planning to make and use images, then you must be cine-literate.

You must be able to identify and describe shots as well as being able to critically show what those techniques mean and how they contribute to a film beyond the basics of the narrative. After all, this is the narration itself; you wouldn't read a book without thinking about the author's word choices and use of grammar.

EXERCISE

The long take
Think about your favourite long take. Now try to work out how you could present the same sequence with multiple shots and editing. Would this add extra meaning to the sequence? How would the meanings of the sequence change?

**In the Mood for Love
(dir: Wong Kar-Wai 2000)**

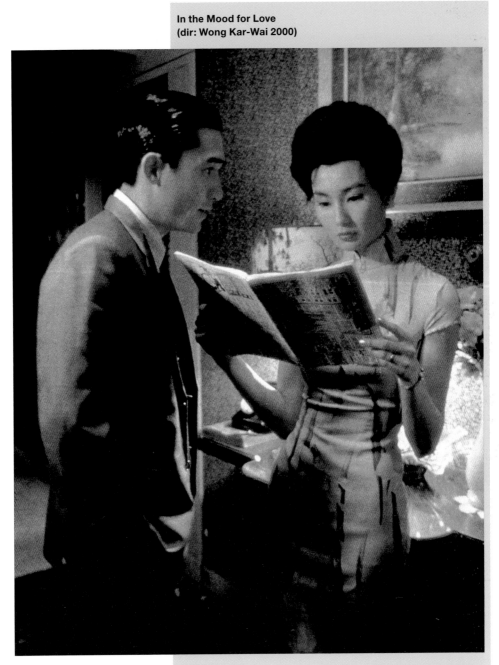

Wong Kar-Wai's use of slow motion in *In the Mood for Love* gives sequences a dreamlike quality as time slows and the moments the couple steal together stretch into eternity.

The mobile camera frame > **Time and the long take** > Case study: Without Tyres

CASE STUDY

Without Tyres
Elephant Productions

Director | Joe Perry

Screenwriter | Rob Weber

Cast including | Matthew Meakin (Dave)
Eddie Rex (Benson)
Barry Woods (Phillip)
Daz Kaye (Paul Boye)
Steve O'Mally (Vernon)

Crew including | Carl Thompson (cinematographer)
Paul Sutcliffe (editor)
Andrew Scrivener (production design)
Luke O'Brien (sound editor)

Tagline | The wrong guys, in the wrong place at the wrong time –
and they're only trying to get home.

Without Tyres: Opening montage

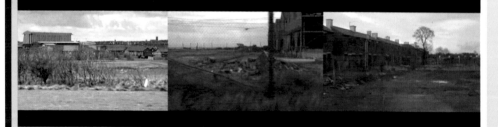

The opening series of tracking shots, all moving left to right,
immediately inscribes the film with the theme of travel. The *mise en
scène* is one of squalor and urban degradation. Although not part
of the story, this sequence is important in establishing the tone and
mood of the film.

Frames and images

Synopsis

Take a look at *Without Tyres*, which is available at www.avabooks. ch/index.php/ava/bookdetails/978-2-940411-27-6. Dave and Benson visit Paul Boye to rent a car. Soon, their trip is interrupted by a noise coming from the boot of the car. When they investigate, they discover a body, a living body! Meanwhile, Paul is having a problem with a local gangster – he's only gone and rented the car with the body in the boot. What will Dave and Benson do with the man in the boot? Can Paul find them in time to save his own skin?

We can use Joe Perry's film to show how different shots, compositions and *mise en scène* can be used to add visual detail to the narrative. The plot of the film is fairly sketchy, but the story is rich in detail, especially the use of locations and the moody, high-key black-and-white photography.

Style is content

The opening sequence of the film does two things:

- Establishes tone.
- Creates a motif.

The black-and-white photography, combined with the images of urban squalor, tells us that this will be a dark film – really it's a dark comedy. Using images of run-down factories and derelict housing creates a theme of poverty and degradation; it's this environment that allows the main gangster to prosper and thrive. Whether intentional or not, this is a political statement.

These travelling shots also establish a motif. Travelling is a key theme in the film. Rather than just being a purely narrative theme, the tracking shots inscribe travel into the visuals, becoming particularly apparent in shots such as a train passing or the car in motion. It's once the action stops travelling that the trouble begins. You might also notice that the tracking shots tend to stop or become less frequent when the two protagonists aren't on the move.

It's also important to remember that this sequence is not in any way related to the narrative of the film; it's purely tonal and thematic.

Pacing

One of the things that we can see in the montage of shots from the film is the development of motifs. Perry uses two-shots to put his two protagonists into a balanced relationship. These shots are generally composed in a balanced way, the two protagonists aren't differentiated, and neither takes more power than the other in the relationship.

As the narrative becomes tenser, and they find the body in the boot of the car, Perry begins to use bigger and tighter close-ups. This emphasises reactions and emotions for the viewer, increasing the tension visually, as the tension in the narrative builds. The motif is linked to the pacing of the film, which builds as the shots become tighter and closer.

Long establishing shot

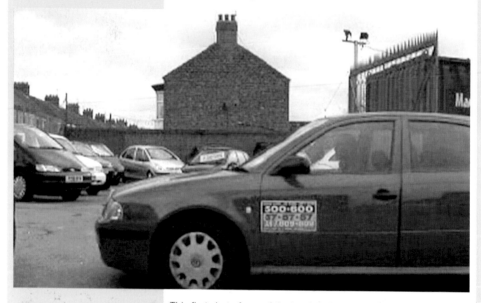

This first shot of one of the key locations quickly alerts the viewer to where the action takes place: a car dealership. The protagonists arrive in a taxi, signalling to the viewer, simply, that they don't have their own car. This is clearly indicated in the *mise en scène*.

Establishing a motif – two-shots

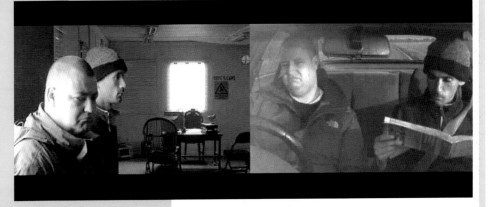

The film tends to use a lot of two-shot medium close-ups for views of the protagonists; this distributes power between them equally.

Mise en scène

Mise en scène is obviously present in all of the shots of the film, but some are more expressive than others.

For example, the viewer's introduction to the gangster is handled by showing him first as an ominous dark shadow on the wall, a tonal element, well aided by the black-and-white photo imagery. Meanwhile, the sleazy car dealer is introduced in the background, reminding us that he's an untrustworthy, shady character, aided by the casting, but also eventually established in the narrative and dialogue. However, it's immediately established visually.

The raised bridge is also an important symbol, effectively stalling the narrative by halting the movement of the two main characters. From here on in, the film tends to use fewer moving shots as the motif of travelling is diminished.

Repetition with difference

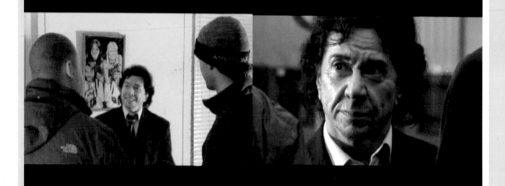

By locating him behind the protagonists, our sleazy car dealer is diminished in this composition; he's smaller than our protagonists and lurking in the background. Later in the film, a similar shot is framed much closer, but arranged similarly. This difference in the repeated shot reminds us of the earlier shot and how the dynamic of the narrative has now changed.

Frames and images

The scale of the problem

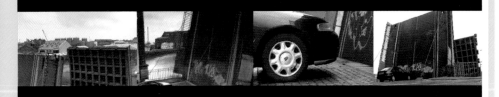

Continuing the theme of movement in the film, the camera cranes down and pans from the top of the open bridge to the protagonists' car, thus stressing the size of the bridge and the problem that confronts them. Subsequent shots reinforce this, using close-ups to emphasise the car stopping or low-angle shots to stress the size of the bridge in comparison to the car.

Introducing the villain

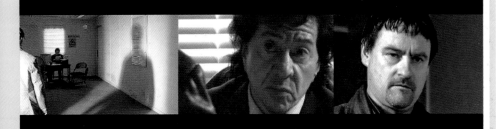

The sequence that introduces the villain is shot with low-key lighting that is ominous and menacing. His power is also reinforced with a low-angle shot that looks down on the car dealer, who is anxiously framed in a tight, dark close-up.

'Cutting' toward a conclusion

After discovering the body in the boot of the car, the two protagonists discuss how to deal with it. We're shown a fantasy sequence with percussive, pacey music. The sequence is shot hand-held for greater energy, while there is a much greater use of tight close-ups than in the rest of the film. It's a good example of how the film-maker has changed their style for a specific effect.

As the narrative further intensifies toward its conclusion and the film becomes more driven by its dialogue, the director uses more close-ups than previously, although not as close or energetic as in the fantasy sequence. This tends to emphasise key lines of dialogue and reactions, and to increase pace, as this means more cutting than earlier in the film, where more smooth tracking shots were used.

Close analysis

Breaking a film apart like this can let us see why a director has chosen to use certain shots for key points in the narrative, how relationships between shots are created and altered, how tone and pace are established, and how meaning is added to the narrative.

Try doing this with any film to see just how much the camera adds to the material it captures.

Increasing pace

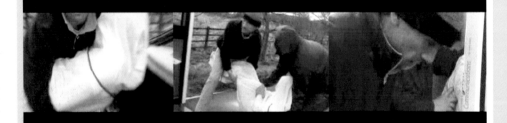

The pacing for this fantasy sequence is noticeably different to the rest of the film.

Leaving the scene

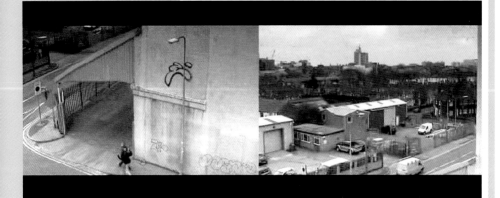

In the film's final shot, our two protagonists leave the scene of their little incident. The camera follows them in long shot, making them seem insignificant. The shot then tilts up and pans to give us a final shot of the city, which looks as grim as earlier in the film. This returns us full circle visually; the narrative is resolved but nothing has really changed.

DISCUSSION QUESTIONS

Reading *Without Tyres* is an exercise in working with the grammar of film. What for you is the difference between reading semiotics and reading film structure?

Analysing scenes allows you to identify the multiple camera shots utilised to create an effect. Why do films need to use anything other than a static camera? Consider this in relation to *Without Tyres*.

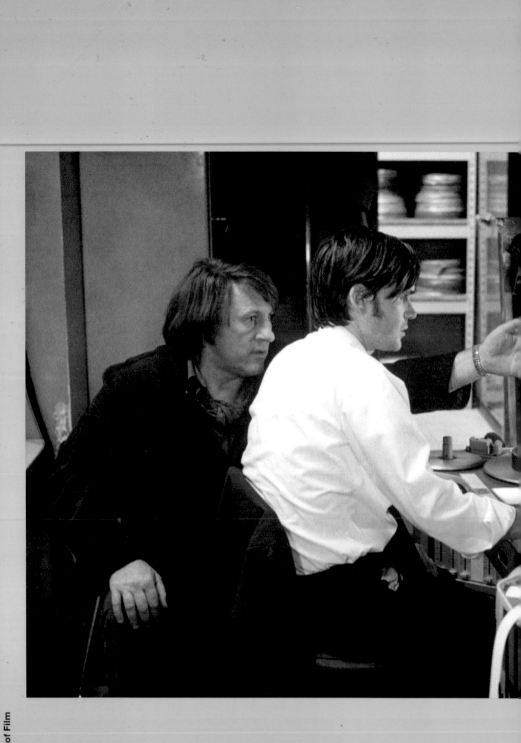

CONSTRUCTING MEANING

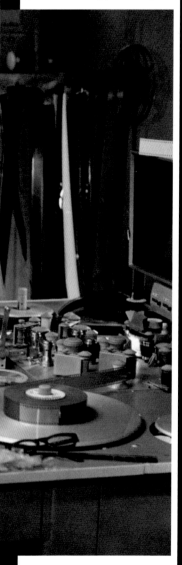

One of the most significant debates throughout the history of film has been the battle between the formalists and the realists. The formalists thought film was an abstract art form based on artistic principles of composition and manipulation. The realists argued that film was a reflection of our material reality, like photography, although with the capacity for recording movement. At the heart of this battle was editing.

There were those, such as André Bazin, who felt editing added little, and reminded the audience that they were watching a film; he preferred the long take. Others, such as Sergei Eisenstein, saw cinema as montage, as a construction that was intellectual and dialectical. Throughout the 1920s he battled with his Russian contemporaries, such as Vsevolod Pudovkin, who saw editing as a series, a progression of continuous shots.

Meanwhile, on the other side of the world, D. W. Griffith had developed what we now know as continuity editing, a logical, coherent and psychologically dramatic mode of editing that remains the dominant mode of editing today in both film and television.

As ever, film is a construction of hundreds of individual shots. The skill of the editor is to construct a coherent whole out of this material.

Continuity editing

Glossary

Jump cuts: The term jump cut can be used in two ways. First, it can refer to a shot that is arrhythmic or disjunctive and produces a noticeable skip between two shots, either because action isn't matched or the shots break the 30° rule. Most commonly, though, jump cuts refer to cuts that interrupt a single shot, literally producing a jump.

Master (or establishing) shot: Often the first shot of a scene, the master, usually a long shot, shows the viewer the whole scene, the setting, spatial relationships between characters and important action. Sometimes, whole scenes are shot 'in masters'.

Continuity is the dominant style of editing used by film-makers. It has developed over more than a century as a way in which space, time and narrative can be constructed out of hundreds of fragments to form a coherent, logical and continuous whole. It allows two shots that might have been filmed months apart, in different locations, to be cut together following a pattern of established rules to suggest they happened one after another.

The rules

Continuity has often been criticised as a conservative method of film-making. It slavishly follows rules and presents the viewer with an image of the world that is ordered, coherent and structured.

Of course, the real world doesn't function this way but film audiences have been conditioned to accept these editing rules as dominant, hegemonic even, so that any deviation from this pattern looks 'wrong' and shatters the illusion. Of course, some film-makers want to achieve this effect, but we'll leave that until the next section.

Continuity editing follows a series of rules that fulfil several purposes:

- To tell a story. Everything must be used to tell the story. It is economical, and anything unnecessary must be cut out, while repetition must be minimised.
- To construct and preserve a coherence of space.
- To maintain a continuity of time.
- To create and sustain graphic and rhythmic relations.
- To hide the means of construction from the viewer.

The cliché goes that, like film music, editing is successful when the viewer doesn't notice it. Pacing is maintained, there are no **jump cuts** and the sense of space and time is preserved. If the viewer notices a cut, then the editor has failed. This, largely, is nonsense.

Continuity editing is a style, albeit a realist one, but the editor does not need to slavishly follow rules. Art can be subversive and it is often in breaking the rules that the artist makes his or her trade. If you see a film in which the editing is visible, don't immediately think that it's just a mistake, but try to think why the film-maker has included that cut and what it means.

Continuity editing has a number of 'rules' that need to be observed to preserve either temporal or spatial continuity, these are:

- The 180° rule
- Match-on-action
- Eyeline matches
- The 30° rule
- Shot-reverse-shot editing

A typical scene edited in this style will follow a similar pattern. The scene will begin with a **master shot**; this will often be a long shot that establishes the basic spatial pattern for the scene. From here, the editor will cut closer into the action. If it is a dialogue-driven scene, there may be a combination of two-shot medium close-ups from the waist up or close-ups for important lines of dialogue and reactions. An action scene will tend to use more close-ups. Modern action scenes will often use montage principles of metric or rhythmic pacing for impact.

The 180° rule

The 180° rule is intended to preserve spatial continuity in a sequence. When the sequence is shot, the director will observe an imaginary 180° line across which he or she will not cross.

For example, if in one shot, a character is walking left to right and exits frame right, the character must enter the next shot from frame left and continue to walk left to right. If the director places the camera on the other side of the action, the action will be inverted; even if the location is the same and the character is walking in the same direction, when cut together the actor will appear to be walking in the opposite direction, thereby breaking spatial continuity and confusing the audience.

Match-on-action

Like the 180° rule, the match-on-action is used to preserve spatial continuity. However, it is also used to show the temporal progression of the action. If the character in the previous example encountered a door, the action would need to be matched across shots. The first shot would show the actor opening the door and beginning to walk through. The next would show the actor coming through the door without repeating the door opening or skipping part of the action.

If the action is not matched, the cut would be visible, producing a noticeable jump. This is fine if you want to call attention to the cut for an artistic purpose, but not if you want to show a smooth, flowing action.

Tip

A violation of the 180° rule is known as 'crossing the line'. This can sometimes be avoided by inserting a buffer shot from a head-on angle to make the transition to the other side.

Things to look out for

Watch the car chase at the factory in *Goldfinger* (dir: Guy Hamilton 1964); look out for a moment where Bond's car crosses the line. Why do you think the director has included this? It's not just because the footage didn't edit together, so what is its effect?

Recommended reading

Ken Dancyger's *The Technique of Film and Video Editing* (2006) is a comprehensive exploration of the role of the editor and the style, history and technique of editing.

Eyeline matches

Eyeline matches are another important device used to preserve spatial coherence.

Imagine our actor again: they've entered a new room and we see them look off frame right, slightly down. In the next shot, we see another actor; they're looking at our first actor. This second actor needs to be looking slightly upwards toward the eyeline of the first actor. This is an important point of continuity. The lines must match to show that the two actors aren't just staring off into space. Of course, they probably haven't been looking at each other on the set, but the matched cut constructs that relationship.

The same would be true of a point of view (POV) shot from our actor's perspective. If he is looking downwards out of frame, the subjective shot that follows would need to tilt down to match that eyeline.

If you want to see an example of how this important continuity rule isn't followed, just watch Ed Wood's *Plan 9 from Outer Space* (1959), notoriously regarded as the worst film of all time. Wood and his editor don't follow any of the conventional rules of continuity.

The 30° rule

The 30° rule is a simple, but important, rule that editors and directors must remember. If shot angles differ by less than 30°, the cut will produce a noticeable jump as the angles are too similar to be cut together.

Again, this doesn't stop directors breaking the rule. For example, François Truffaut breaks this rule in *Shoot the Pianist* (1960) when he uses a triple cut (cutting closer and closer within the same shot like a zoom) of a character hovering over a door bell, but choosing not to ring it. The jumpy cut says a lot about the fragmented, hesitant state of mind of our protagonist (an example of expressionism).

The secret to film is that it's an illusion.

George Lucas, producer, screenwriter and director

**Cheap Beans
(dir: Martyn Johnston 2008)**

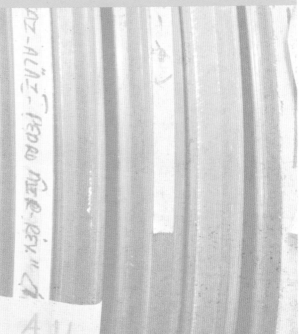

This cut is matched on action: the girl turns her head and moves upwards into shot. The cut matches on that action, as she continues to turn into the second shot.

Glossary

Cutaways: Shot-reverse-shot might also include shots of a character reacting to a line of dialogue; shots like these are known as cutaways, or, in TV, 'noddies'.

Shot-reverse-shot editing

Shot-reverse-shot editing is the 'meat and potatoes' of continuity editing. It's where all the rules come together.

Following the 180° rule and principles of continuity, shot-reverse-shot editing refers to the back-and-forth method often used for conversations and reaction shot **cutaways**. To return to our two actors who have now met: they strike up a conversation. The cutting of close-ups would be as follows:

- Shot one: Actor one, framed to left of frame in medium close-up (MCU) looking toward frame right.
- Shot two: Actor two, framed to right of frame in MCU looking toward frame left.
- Shot three: as shot one.
- Shot four: as shot two (and so on).

This pattern will preserve the coherence of space. If we were to flip shot two, it would appear the same as shot one and would have crossed the line. This would make the actors appear to be either in the same place or talking away from each other. Either way, space would be shattered and the images would look too similar, producing a jump cut by violating the 30° rule.

Missing reverse shot

Shot-reverse-shot can also be used to hide things and trouble the viewer. For example, *Halloween* (dir: John Carpenter 1978) begins with a long hand-held sequence in which the viewer witnesses a brutal murder from someone's perspective (the action is shown through mask holes – it's an obvious POV shot). The viewer isn't offered a reverse shot for a long time. It is troubling not to know who is committing this horrific crime. As such, the viewer is implicated in the murder as a voyeur.

Carpenter only inserts (or 'sutures') a subject into the subjective shot with the final reverse shot – when the viewer is shown the six-year old Michael Myers. Carpenter could have included a reverse shot much earlier to provide us with this information, but he decides not to. The viewer naturally wants to know who the murderer is, but this information is withheld until the end of the sequence. It is typical of the horror film to withhold narrative information from the viewer by avoiding reverse shots for POVs. Part of the pleasure of the horror film is identifying with monsters and villains; the missing reverse shot can help make this possible.

Without Wires (dir: Alex Woodcock 2008)

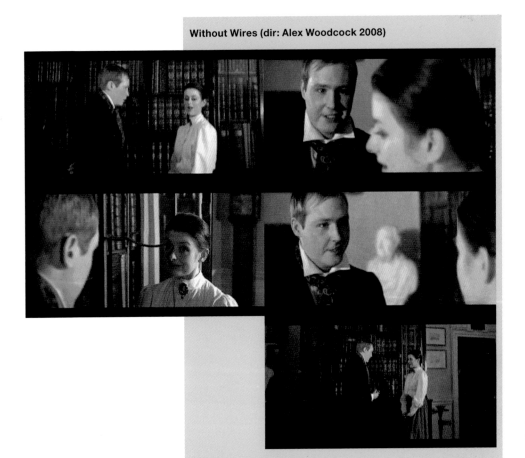

In this brief sequence, we see a good example of shot-reverse-shot organisation. After the initial establishing shot, we follow shot-reverse-shot, back and forth between the actors' dialogue before returning to another two-shot. Notice how the camera does not cross the line, the action preserves a continuous line of action and eyelines match between shots.

Intensified continuity

David Bordwell has noted that the standard continuity style has intensified since the 1960s, becoming dominant in the 1980s. The intensified style of continuity is still rooted in the traditional premises of spatial continuity. However, Bordwell finds that this modern style of continuity tends to use fewer master shots than previous examples, which re-establish space when characters move. The style is also marked by:

- more editing
- more and tighter close-ups
- more shots overall, especially of reactions
- use of longer lenses, producing tight long shots
- fewer medium shots

Rather than turning toward a greater montage style, Bordwell sees these changes as an intensification of the existing style rather than a change in pattern. The new rule is more, tighter and faster.

EXERCISE

Reading the edit

Choose a five-minute sequence in a narrative film. Explore the editing of the sequence. Try to look for the ways in which the editor follows the rules of continuity editing, especially graphic and eyeline matches. Are there any moments where those rules aren't followed? If there are, what is the consequence of those moments?

Transitions

There are a number of common devices that an editor can use to imply ellipses (cuts in which material is implied as missing). Similarly, these devices can be used to suggest jumps in time and space:

- **Dissolves:** a smooth transition from one shot to another.
- **Fades:** a transition from one shot to another with a fade to black (or other colour), and fade into the second shot.
- **Wipes:** a line wipes one shot from the screen, which is replaced by the next.
- **Irises:** a circular frame closes on one shot and opens on another, often isolating an important detail; irises were commonly used in silent cinema for emphasis.
- **Freeze frames:** the frame may freeze before a transition or can stop time for emphasis. Often an arty technique.

Unlike straight cuts, most of the above are 'soft' transitions and are less jarring for the viewer.

Similarly, graphic matches are edits that create visual relationships between shots. They often emphasise thematic or spatial relationships between objects/subjects. For instance, in *2001: A Space Odyssey* (1968), Stanley Kubrick uses a single cut to show the viewer the history of human evolution. The 'Dawn of Man' prologue ends with a shot of an ape throwing a bone in the air. The bone spins and begins to fall, at which point Kubrick cuts to a shot of a spaceship drifting through space. The movement and shape of the two objects is matched graphically, stressing a thematic relationship between the first tool and the invention of space travel. It is all done in a single cut.

Recommended viewing

Watch *Star Wars* (dir: George Lucas 1977) and see how many different kinds of transitions are used to move from one scene to another smoothly. This is a motif used throughout the series and its spin-offs.

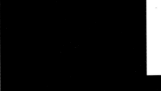

Film editing is now something almost everyone can do at a simple level and enjoy it, but to take it to a higher level requires the same dedication and persistence that any art form does.

Walter Murch, film editor and sound designer

Continuity editing > Discontinuity editing

Discontinuity editing, as its name suggests, is the opposite of continuity editing. Although it sometimes uses the same devices, such as graphic matches, it is not concerned with the narrative experience of cinema. As such, it tends to use devices that subvert or disrupt the coherence of space and time in a film.

Discontinuity outside the mainstream

Discontinuity techniques are popular in avant-garde or art films where narrative is not the main concern of the film-maker. Editing will often refer to character psychology, graphic and rhythmic relationship, or comment on the ideological form of the medium.

Many of the techniques of discontinuity editing have now also found their way into the mainstream. Montage and graphic matching are common in music videos, where narrative takes a backseat to the music, or in action films to give images impact to physically affect the viewer.

Un Chien Andalou (dir: Luis Buñuel 1929) is probably the most famous avant-garde film ever made. Using a series of discontinuous editing techniques to fragment space and critique the devices of continuity, the film subverts narrative flow, and confronts the logic of space and time. It takes the form of a **surreal** dream about sexual, political and religious themes.

Fragmenting space

The opening sequence of *Un Chien Andalou* is a perfect example of how avant-garde films use discontinuity editing without concern for presenting the viewer with a coherent narrative. The shots can be broken down as follows:

1 An intertitle that reads 'Once Upon a Time...'.

2 A close-up, from an elevated angle, looking down at a man's hand sharpening a razor. The man's arms are framed toward the frame right.

3 A medium close-up: the man with a cigarette in his mouth looks down, presumably at the razor. He is framed toward frame left. Spatially, in relation to the previous shot, the man must be on the left side of the razor sharpener, not the right, as in the previous shot.

4 Return to Shot 2: the man tests the sharpness of the razor against the back of his thumbnail.

5 A medium long shot: the man folds up the razor and the sharpener, opens the balcony window and begins to leave.

6 Matched on action: the man walks out onto the balcony in another medium long shot. He stands for a moment and then leans on the balcony.

7 Medium close up: the man looks up toward frame left.

8 Long shot: a POV of the moon in the sky.

9 Return to Shot 7.

10 Close-up of a woman's face. A man, standing just to her right, pulls open her left eye and puts the razor toward it. This man, unlike the man we've already seen, wears a tie.

11 Return to Shot 8: a cloud drifts across the moon.

12 In extreme close-up: the razor slices an eyeball open.

13 An intertitle that reads '8 Years Later'.

This sequence displays some of the key principles of discontinuity editing:

- A lack of concern for logical temporal progression: the intertitles make no sense, they are arbitrary and the man in the opening sequence never returns.

- Little interest in coherent spatial relationships: the man clearly swaps sides of the razor while sharpening it.

- An obsession with graphic matches: the cloud drifting across the moon is graphically matched with the slicing of the eyeball.

- Surreal logic and dream states: the eyeball slicing is a daydream, and the progression of the narrative is alogical (not just illogical, but lacking logic altogether).

Lack of narrative

As the list of shots shows, discontinuity editing may use some of the same devices as continuity editing, such as shot-reverse-shot, match-on-action and graphic matches, but there is little or no concern for narrative. Instead the film-makers are concerned with using the medium to explore subjective mental states and to investigate the artistic properties of the medium.

Discontinuity editing could be thought of as 'bad' editing because it breaks the rules of continuity editing. However, we need to consider why film-makers might break those rules and what meanings are uncovered by their transgressions.

Recommended viewing

Jean-Luc Godard mixes realist long takes and discontinuity editing in *Breathless* (1960) to create a contrast of styles. Notice how jump cuts are used as a distancing device to remind the viewer of the unnaturalness of the film text and the arbitrary rules that govern most continuity editing.

Continuity editing > **Discontinuity editing** > Montage

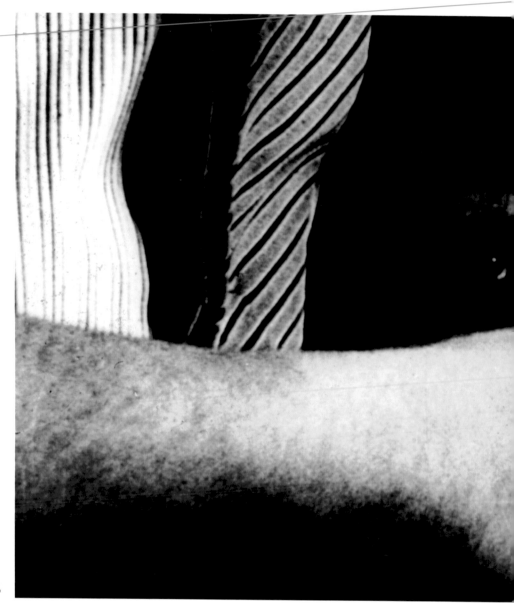

**Un Chien Andalou
(dir: Luis Buñuel 1929)**

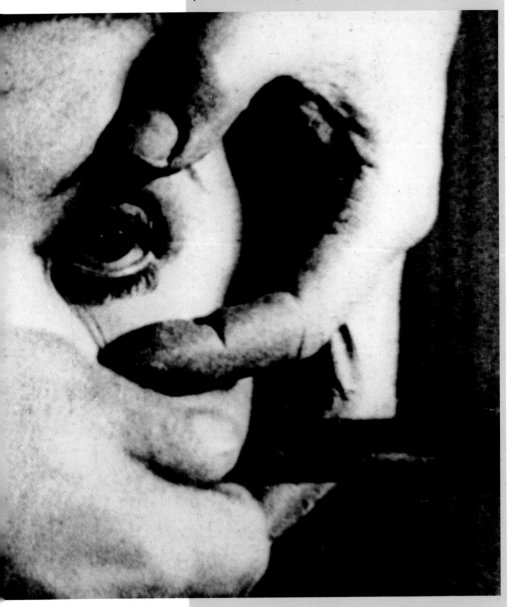

As one of the most important and significant avant-garde films, *Un Chien Andalou* can show us how discontinuity is used to fracture a film's space. The slicing of the eyeball is also a visual pun on editing as cutting.

Recommended viewing

Alfred Hitchcock is famous for several of his montage sequences. The most famous is the shower sequence in *Psycho* (1960), in which Hitchcock uses montage to imply violence. The viewer never sees the knife enter the body. All of the cuts are filmic. Try watching this sequence again and think about how the editing makes you think you see things that aren't really there.

Derived from the French verb *monter*, meaning 'to assemble', montage is a general term for editing in film. However, it is now most often used to describe a particular mode of intellectual or non-realist editing that creates meaning out of unrelated material. Montage is heavily associated with the Soviet school of film-making of the 1920s and 1930s, although many of the principles developed by those film-makers have found their way into mainstream cinema.

The Kuleshov experiment

Lev Kuleshov was a Soviet pioneer of montage. He conducted an experiment in which he took a shot of an impassive actor's face and cut it together with shots of emotive material: a plate of food; a child's body lying in a coffin. The montage effect was such that viewers thought the actor was expressing an emotion even though he had no expression on his face. Cutting the face together with the food connoted hunger for instance. The actor was even praised for his performance!

This experiment, although the original footage is long lost, has had long-lasting repercussions for film-makers, especially concerning actors' performances. Film acting is often subtle, with emotional effects created in editing.

The Kuleshov experiment

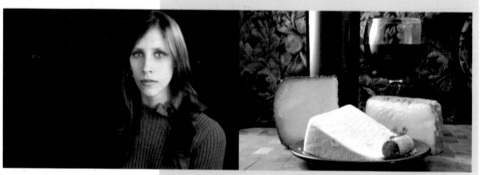

Although Kuleshov's original experiment no longer exists, we can approximate it. Putting these two images together suggests a relationship between them, implying the woman is looking at the food and therefore hungers for it.

Montage sequences

Montage can also be used to describe a sequence that condenses narrative information into a short sequence of linked shots, often set to music. Wes Anderson uses this technique in *Rushmore* (2000) and *The Royal Tenenbaums* (2001) to quickly give the viewer narrative details in a fast and snappy way.

Perhaps the best-known sequence of this kind is a spoof in *Team America: World Police* (dir: Trey Parker 2004), a parody of training montages in films such as *Rocky* (dir: John G. Avildsen 1976), set to a pulsating rock song called 'Montage!'

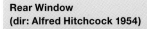

**Rear Window
(dir: Alfred Hitchcock 1954)**

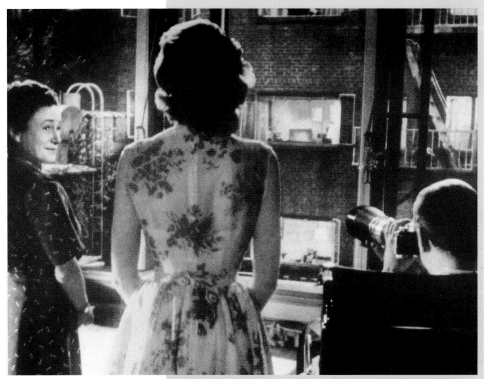

Hitchcock once said the best actors were good at doing nothing. James Stewart's performance in *Rear Window* is minimal, with effects often created, Kuleshov-style, in the montage effect between his face and what he is looking at.

Discontinuity editing > **Montage** > Sound editing and filmic space

Recommended reading

Eisenstein's own writing is the main body of writing on montage. *Film Form: Essays in Film Theory* (1969) is the most significant work of Eisenstein's regarding the development of montage, as well as his theories on film sound. Additionally, you should also look at Eisenstein's films for demonstrations of his technique, as these are discussed in his writings.

Glossary

Dialectic: The opposition between two conflicting forces or elements.

Sergei Eisenstein

Undoubtedly, the master of montage was Sergei Eisenstein. Eisenstein developed his theories of attractional, agitational montage in the theatre following the Russian Revolution of 1917. He believed the business of film was conflict of all kinds: of lines, angles, colours and ideas.

The most significant mode of montage is **dialectical** or intellectual. Here, the film-maker takes two unrelated ideas and cuts them together to make a thematic or intellectual point. In *Strike* (1925), Eisenstein inserts non-diegetic shots of cattle being slaughtered into scenes of workers being massacred by government forces. The thematic point created makes a point about the mistreatment of collective groups, an important ideological concern in post-revolution Russia. Francis Ford Coppola uses the same cross-cutting technique in *Apocalypse Now* (1979) to juxtapose the murder of Colonel Kurtz with the killing of a cow, to comment on abuses of power.

The basic premise of Eisenstein's method was a vulgar Marxist notion of dialecticism, derived from Lenin. His equation was simple:

Thesis + Antithesis = Synthesis

Montage came in the moment of synthesis. This is where the intellectual concept was created, in the conflict between two opposing ideas. There's nothing particularly subtle about this method, nor was it intended to be: 'It is not a cine-eye that we need,' claimed Eisenstein, 'but a cine-fist.'

Eisenstein developed several other modes of montage that were intended to produce emotional, thematic and visual resonances in a film:

- Metric: lengths of shots are determined by factors not depicted in the image, such as musical time signatures. Not favoured by Eisenstein, but still popular in music videos, and used by Martin Scorsese at the beginning of *Mean Streets* (1973), where a triple-cut is cut to the beginning of 'Be My Baby' by The Ronettes.
- Rhythmic: similar to metric montage, but the rhythm of shots is determined by material in the shots themselves. The 'Odessa Steps' sequence in Eisenstein's *Battleship Potemkin* (1925) was an experiment in rhythmic montage, with the shots getting shorter as the action in the sequence accelerated. This is mimicked in *The Untouchables* (dir: Brian De Palma 1987).
- Tonal: montage determined by the dominant emotional tone of the sequence. The fog rolling into the port in Potemkin is one of the key examples of this form of montage in Eisenstein's work.
- Overtonal: the conflict between different types of the above montage effects. Darren Aronofsky creates some very aggressive and distressing effects from overtonal montage in *Requiem for a Dream* (2000).

**Battleship Potemkin
(dir: Sergei Eisenstein 1925)**

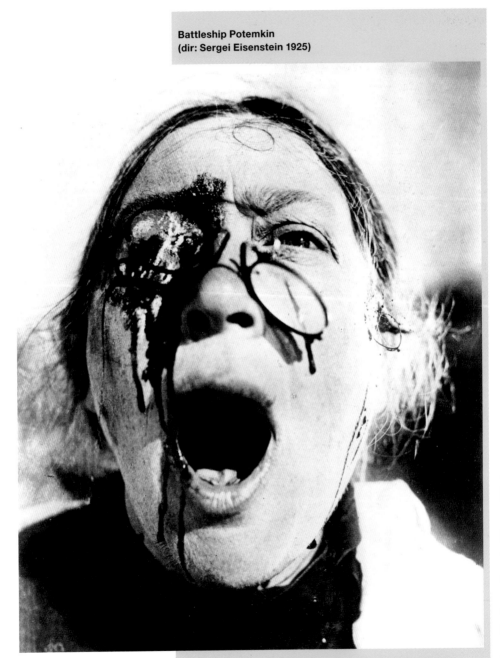

The 'Odessa steps' sequence in *Battleship Potemkin* is an experiment in rhythmic editing. Eisenstein uses the pace of the editing to show the acceleration of the action. He also uses editing to signify violence; we don't see the act of violence, which is implied in the cut.

Discontinuity editing > **Montage** > Sound editing and filmic space

Glossary

Asynchronous sound: That which does not match the image. It might be dubbed dialogue that doesn't match the on-screen lip movements; a dog might miaow. Alternatively, synchronous sound is that which is heard at the same time that it is produced in the diegesis, for example dialogue or gun shots. Synchronised sound can be on-screen or off and is in time with the image.

So far we've looked at how film images are edited to create a filmic space, whether coherent or not. However, although we often take it for granted, sound is one of the most important parts of film's overall aesthetic design. Sound, just as much as anything visual, can create convincing realist spaces, or distort and subvert realism.

Sound and space

Sound can give an audience the illusion of a 360° world. Often, film sound can seem spatialised and directed, so the audience might hear dialogue perfectly, even if characters are speaking in a noisy environment like a nightclub or a crowded restaurant. The dialogue might also be louder or quieter depending on how close the characters are to the camera. Sound would be prioritised due to the narrative's requirements. Therefore, sound has perspective, just as vision does.

Sound can roughly be broken down into two categories: diegetic and non-diegetic.

Diegetic (or actual) sound refers to any sound emanating from the fictional world (the diegesis) within the film, including:

- character's voices
- sound effects, both on- and off-screen
- music that can be identified as coming from a diegetic source such as jukeboxes, instruments and so on.

Non-diegetic (or commentary) sound refers to anything that does not emanate from the fictional world, including:

- voice-over narration
- dramatic or imagined sound effects
- a musical score or soundtrack.

This is not to be confused with live or post-production sound. Diegetic sound can, and usually is, added in post-production. Some cinemas have traditionally worked entirely with post-synchronised sound, especially in Italy and Hong Kong.

Sound quality

In *Film Art: An Introduction* (1979) David Bordwell and Kristin Thompson identify a series of qualities that film sound exhibits:

- Acoustic properties:
  - loudness
  - pitch
  - timbre
- Dimensions of sound:
  - rhythm
  - fidelity
  - space
  - time

All film sounds will exhibit these seven qualities. In *Ringu* (dir: Hideo Nakata 1998), the sound of the cursed videotape is manipulated for pitch and timbre to sound metallic, scratchy and to affect the audience physically. Other films, such as David Lynch's *Mulholland Drive* (2001), play with the fidelity of sound – its time and space. This helps the audience question the sounds used and to explore the lack of reality in the relationship between film and its soundtrack.

Recommended reading

Sound Practice, Sound Theory (1992) is a collection of essays edited by Rick Altman that looks at the technique, theory and history of film sound. Each essay discusses a different aspect or type of film sound, from the sound of cartoons to the recording of women's voices.

Tip

Asynchronous sound is often exploited for artistic or comic effect, as in *Singin' in the Rain* (dir: Stanley Donen and Gene Kelly 1952) when an early sound film goes out of synch. This technique usually reminds the audience that they are watching a film.

EXERCISE

Listening to the soundtrack

Try watching a sequence from one of your favourite films with your eyes closed. Listen to the soundtrack closely. How do you get a sense of space just from listening to the soundtrack? Now watch with your eyes open. How does the soundtrack relate to the images? Does the sequence use any non-diegetic or **asynchronous sound**?

Tip

Sound perspective is the apparent direction of sound reverberating in space. Perspective can be suggested by manipulating volume, echo and the balance in relation to other sounds in the diegesis.

Recommended viewing

Watch the first half or so of *Wall-E* (dir: Andrew Stanton 2008) and listen to the ways in which sound is used to tell the story. There is no dialogue, so the narrative needs to be driven in other ways. Try to hear how the acoustic properties and dimensions of sound are manipulated.

Multi-layered sound

Robert Altman developed a very distinctive and realist way of using sound. Altman often directed films with big ensemble casts, from *MASH* (1970) to *Gosford Park* (2001). He recorded sound with radio microphones attached to individual actors. Therefore when we watch one of his films, sound is often cluttered with dialogue from multiple characters (although it was often manipulated). At times, however, we might see characters on-screen, but be listening to dialogue from off-screen. The overall effect was a constant 360° space filled with characters and activity that doesn't stop just because it isn't necessary for the narrative or is off-screen.

EXERCISE

Creating a sequence
Many film-makers consider film to be an editor's art. Film comes alive in editing. Try to think about how shots fit together and how cinema isn't just about the things that we can see.

Now, using all of the knowledge of film aesthetics from the previous two chapters, take a piece of text, a stage play or short story, and create a cinematic sequence. Try to pay attention to how you will tell the story, which shots will work best, how the sequence will cut together and how it will sound. Think about what you are trying to achieve overall: realism? non-realism? expressionism? emotion?

**McCabe and Mrs Miller
(dir: Robert Altman 1971)**

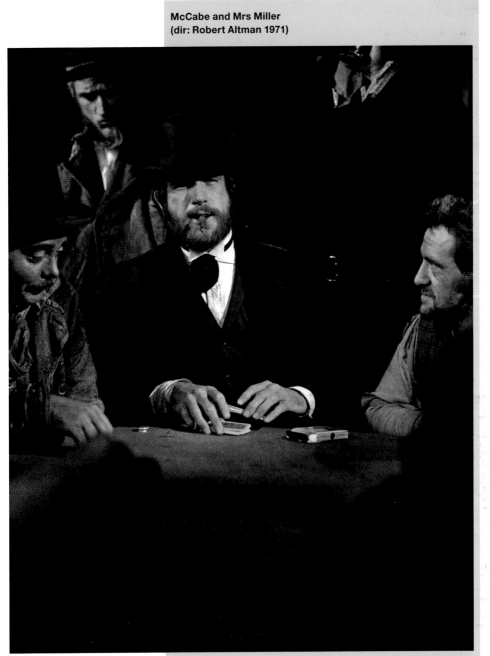

McCabe and Mrs Miller is one of Altman's most distinctive and realist films. It uses multi-layered sound to convey a space beyond the vision of the camera.

CASE STUDY

Tide
Mushroom Cloud Productions

Director	Thomas Swingler
Screenwriter	Thomas Swingler, Ben West, Ian Bell, David Browne
Cast including:	David Lord (Joe) Aimee Parkes (Julie) Kat Wilson (Anna)
Crew including	Matthew Brannan (cinematographer) Dan Nelson (editor) Rachael Smith (production design) Adam Johnston, Thomas Swingler, Ben West (sound mixing)
Tagline	Relationships are built on memory.

Synopsis

Take a look at the short film *Tide* (2003) – available at www.avabooks.ch/index.php/ava/bookdetails/978-2-940411-27-6 . In this short film a young woman, Julie, returns to the house in which she was brought up. The house, however, hides a terrible secret, one that drives Julie to commit murder to protect it.

Tide is very much a mood piece, exploring memory and the past events that haunt us and drive us to desperation.

The sequence explored in this case study is a relatively short one involving Julie (the brunette), her boyfriend Joe and their friend Anna. It features early in the film, just as the main enigma is being set up. Anna and Joe question why he has never met Julie's father and whether anyone has lived in the house for a long time, but Julie tries to leave when questioned, leading to a confrontation between her and Joe, who wants to be taken seriously as her boyfriend. The scene also complicates the relationship between Joe and Anna.

Constructing meaning

Editing tone and performance

There are several important things to notice about this particular sequence. The first thing that is apparent is the emotional intensity; the darkness is enveloping the characters. Even when the scene cuts to a longer shot, the darkness still surrounds the characters. This is partly motivated by realism, as the set is dark and there is only a fire for illumination, but the dark engulfs them, just as Julie's past will. The fire is also highlighted as an important symbol in the *mise en scène*. As the first thing we see, and the bridge between scenes, the editing privileges it as significant tonally and thematically.

The editing also highlights several key features of the characters.

First, you'll notice that there are a number of close-ups and extreme close-ups throughout the sequence. We start on a tight close-up of Julie's eye; the cut implies she's looking at the fire. The symbolism of the cut signifies her emotional temperature. There is also a tight close-up of Anna's eyes when Tom mentions he still hasn't met Julie's father. The reaction shot is ambiguous: is it a desiring glance at Tom? Or is it a knowing look? Does Anna know something about Julie's father? We aren't sure, but the timing and size of the shot signifies its importance.

Secondly, the sequence concentrates on performances. Julie's performance in particular is aided by the choice of shots. In addition to her fairly minimal dialogue, the combination of silence on the sound track (the sound is mostly ambient, the crackling fire and background diegetic music) and the use of close-ups makes Julie's actions in the sequence quite ambiguous. What is she thinking? Is she hiding a secret? Where is her father (as it transpires, he *is* in the house after all)?

This sequence from *Tide* is logical, coherent and focused on its drama and its placement in the narrative. The scene is developing an enigma. Little information is revealed to us through the dialogue, although we learn much about the characters and their relationships, mostly from the little glances that the director and editor have chosen to include. We learn more about the characters than we do about the narrative.

Tip

Many editors cut on emotion, selecting the best takes of performances to construct a sequence around. This sequence from *Tide* is very much focused on performances – observe how important the characters' eyes are.

Sound editing and filmic space > **Case study: Tide**

Constructing space and drama

This short sequence provides a good example of how editing constructs sequences emotionally and tonally. While it mostly uses continuity editing, we also see an example of tonal montage to establish the emotional temperature of the sequence.

Breaking a sequence down like this can help us understand how shots fit together spatially, and also how choices made in editing can help us understand more than just what we see in the shots.

Editing is the unseen element of film aesthetics. We perceive it, but we don't see it. Notice several things about the construction of the sequence:

- There is no establishing shot for the scene; instead there is a dissolve from an interior shot of Julie to the screen being dominated by the fire. This is a thematic point of contact between Julie's turbulent past and the roaring fire; it is a moment of tonal montage.

Extreme close-up

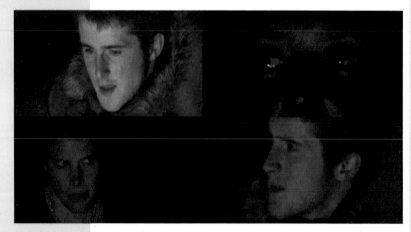

Anna's eyes are framed in extreme close-up after a key line of dialogue. What is she thinking? Is it a shared secret with Julie, or a glance at Tom? What does the relationship of shots suggest?

- The use of eyeline matches to establish space. Notice how characters' eyes follow a logical and coherent line of sight between shots – we understand who is looking at who and therefore can see the conflicts between characters.
- There is one instance of matching on action: Julie gets up to walk past Joe; just as she does, we cut to the wider shot. It is here that we see Joe confront Julie about her father, her past and his need to be taken seriously.
- The scene fades out at the end, signifying a passing of time.
- Shots of Julie and Anna concentrate heavily on their eyes to highlight reactions and to signify elements of their relationship. In this way, the editor and director concentrate heavily on the emotional tone of the scene.
- Even without dialogue, we can see the dramatic construction of the sequence. It is established predominantly in the choice of shots (especially close-ups); the actors' performances, particularly their eyes; the symbolic resonance of the fire, which burns within all of the characters, especially Julie, who murders Joe at the end of the film to protect her family's dark secret.
- The sound is all diegetic – there is no added soundtrack. Music is, we presume, played from a radio on the beach and we can always hear the fire crackling away in the background, continually reminding us of that important symbol.

Tip

Watching any film, try to pay attention to how editing constructs performances from parts, concentrating on the most significant details, such as eyes, hands and mouths. Editing is the actor's friend.

Metaphor

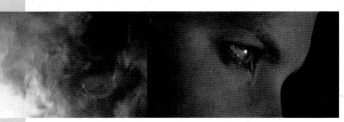

The combination of these two shots implies that Julie is looking at the fire, which acts as a metaphor for her emotional temperature.

The meaning of editing

In most films, the editor constructs the film space (knowledgeable direction will help) from fragments, and turns individual shots into a narrative the audience can understand and a space that is coherent.

This doesn't always need to be the case – film-makers can subvert rules and produce forceful statements about politics and the medium itself by breaking rules.

Like the shots we see, as film-goers we must consider what editing means and how it shapes our experience of film. Only then will we understand how film produces its powerful effect on us.

Shot-reverse-shot sequence

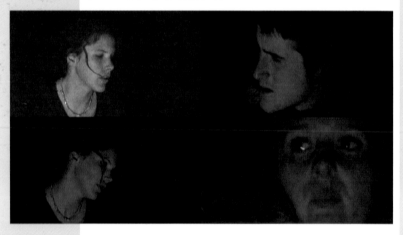

These shots form a simple and conventional shot-reverse-shot sequence; eyelines match, and we never cross the line. Notice though that Julie is framed looser than Tom or Anna, surrounded by more darkness. Why do you think this is?

Concentrating attention

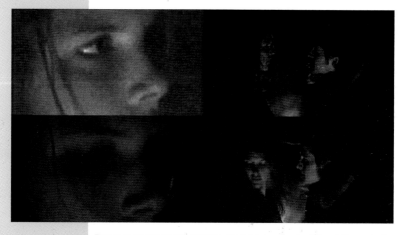

There is no close-up of Tom when he confronts Julie at the end of the scene. This makes him seem powerless, but also concentrates our attention on Julie's reaction with very tight close-ups.

DISCUSSION QUESTIONS

Take any short sequence from a feature film or the whole of a short film such as *Tide* and consider how the editing affects the pace of the film.

Take any film with which you are familiar and look at the transitions between shots. We often discuss meaning as implied, but it is often implied by how images within and across scenes are edited together. How does this work with the examples you have selected?

You have now covered all the basics in understanding the language of film. This is the starting point of knowledge rather than the end of it, and the work continues. For some of you, this will mean putting these ideas into practice by starting the process of making a film. For some of you, it will mean embarking on a career as a theorist or critic. For some of you it will be both. What has been covered here deals with form and content and importantly the relationship between the two. Thus the language of film is not just about *how* film communicates but *what* film communicates.

You will find further reading identified on page 182 You now know which areas interest you the most and which you will find the most useful for your own ends. This is your opportunity to continue your own education and further your knowledge in addition to the instruction provided by any course you might be undertaking. Don't see the recommended reading here as the only information that is available to you; look in libraries, bookshops and on the internet. You will discover that there is no shortage of material around. The lists are broken into introductory and advanced for a reason. There is nothing to stop you starting with a text that is classed as advanced, but don't be put off by the complexity of some of the ideas – you will get it, even if it isn't straight away.

This book has introduced the core theories and ideas that film studies are based upon. The ideas contained in this text intertwine and inform other theories, some of which are specifically about film and others, like ideological analysis, which are broader but which film has adopted and made specific to the medium. These include gender theory, psychoanalytic theory, feminism and apparatus theory.

There are lots of ideas out there and, after all, at root, cinema is about ideas. Happy thinking.

For their contribution and help:

Paul Butler
Graham Cole
Dan Crawforth
Dr Jeff Craine
Keith Wilds

Thanks also to the students and staff of BA Film and
TV Production and MA Film Production at York St John
University for creating such stimulating work.
Also thanks to the students of the University of Kent at
Canterbury, Aberdeen University, Hull University and the
Open University for years of inspiration (and frustration).

Special thanks go to AVA Publishing, in particular
Georgia Kennedy for her expertise and *especially*
her patience.

This book is dedicated to J. R. 'Bob' Dobbs –
this truly is our slack time.

180° rule	Editing rule intended to preserve spatial continuity in a sequence, creating an imaginary line of action that the camera must not cross.
30° rule	Shooting/editing rule; if shot angles differ by less the 30 degrees when cut together the cut will produce a noticeable jump as the angles are too similar to be cut together.
Abstract	To remove (like a dental abstraction) for scrutiny; a concern with form rather than content (as in abstract art).
Aristotle (384–322 BC)	Philosopher and the founding father of textual analysis.
Asynchronous sound	Sound that does not match the image. It might be dubbed dialogue that doesn't match the on-screen lip movements – for example, a dog might miaow.
Auteur	A director whose individual 'vision' is the sole or dominant driving force behind an entire body of work.
Back light	Located behind the subject in three-point lighting to give the subject the appearance of depth by creating a haloing effect around the subject, ensuring the figure won't appear as a flat part of the background.
Barthes, Roland (1915–1980)	Critic responsible for the development of semiotic analysis. His major work, published 1950–70, sought to locate the universal structure and narrative conventions from which the impression of 'meaning' is created in 'realist' texts.
Bullet-time	A digital special effects technique used to slow action, named for the effect in *The Matrix* (1999).
Camera angle	The angle of the camera from the scene being filmed.
Camera height	The physical height of the camera in relation to the actor or object being filmed.
Camera movement	Using a number of methods, from tilting the camera to moving it physically on tracks or a crane, moving the camera adds dramatic effect or simply avoids the need to cut.
Canted (angled) frame	The level of the camera slanted, often to show us a world out of kilter, uncertainty and drama.
Cliché	Overused, stale, and outworn expression – mostly to be avoided, but they are overused for a reason – they tend to *work*, especially when given a slight 'tweak'.
Close-up (CU)	A tightly framed shot that emphasises individual details – faces, hands, feet, small objects – regularly used to give us an insight into significant narrative details.
Continuity editing	The dominant economical style of editing, used to create coherent space and narrative, avoiding unnecessary content and repetition.
Crane (also Helicopter or Airplane) shot	Mounting the camera to a crane can produce stunning shots from great height, either to look down on diminished characters or to show scenery.
Cross-cutting	An editing effect that intertwines narrative threads that are separate in space and/or time, often for the effect of building pace or tension towards a climax.
Crossing the line	A violation of the 180° rule.
Cutaway	Shots of a character reacting to a line of dialogue.
Depth of field (focus)	Focal depth, either shallow, with the background indistinct and out of focus (shot with a long lens) or with everything in focus (deep focus with a short or wide-angle lens).
Dialectic	The opposition between two conflicting forces or elements.
Dialectical (or intellectual) montage	An editing technique that creates a symbolic or thematic association between two unrelated shots.
Dialogic	That what we say always carries something of what has been said in the past, and anticipates something of what will be said in the future.
Diegesis	The fictional story world within the film, the sum of on-screen and off-screen space.
Diegetic	Any object within the fictional world is referred to as diegetic.
Diegetic (or actual) sound	Sound that emanates from characters or objects within the narrative's fictional space, e.g. dialogue, music from jukeboxes, etc.
Discontinuity editing	The opposite of continuity editing, unconcerned with the narrative experience of cinema; the use of editing devices that subvert or disrupt the coherence of space and time in the film, such as unmatched lines of action or symbolic graphic matches.
Dissolve	A smooth transition from one shot to another.
DoP	Director of Photography, head of the camera/lighting department on a film set. In American DP, alternatively cinematographer.

Exposition	The means by which narrative information is relayed to viewers. This can be done visually, but is often conveyed in dialogue, an 'information dump' or a super-villain 'monologuing'.
Expressionism	A style of film-making that uses overt manipulation of image, colour, camera style or *mise en scène* to express inner states of mind of a character or film-maker.
Extreme close-up (XCU)	A very tightly framed shot that isolates very small details – eyes, lips or details of small objects.
Extreme long shot (XLS)	A very long, wide shot that shows us massive backgrounds and tiny, often insignificant people.
Eyeline match	An editing technique that preserves spatial coherence by matching characters' eyelines between shots.
Fade	A transition from one shot to another with a fade to black (or other colour) and fade into the second.
Fill light	Used in three-point lighting; usually positioned on the other side from the key, this light is softer and less bright, which lessens the effect of shadowing on the face.
Film noir	A largely American film genre often based around crime fiction. It has its roots in German Expressionism.
Freeze frame	The frame that stops still before a transition or that stops time for emphasis. Often an arty technique.
Frontality	Action is performed straight-on for the audience, as though on a stage.
Genette, Gérard (1930–present)	French literary theorist and developer of Narratology.
Genre	A French word simply meaning 'type'.
Graphic matches	An edit that creates a visual relationship between shots; often emphasises thematic or spatial relationship between objects/subjects.
Hand-held camera	Similar type of moving shot to the tracking shot, but with a shaky effect that is often associated with a documentary-style realism or with the subjective POV of a character.
High-angle shot	The camera position above the subject, looking down on them. High angles are often used to make the audience feel superior to whatever they are watching.
High-key (high-contrast) lighting	Lighting technique that creates hard shadows combined with bright patches of light common in film noir.
Ideology	A set of ideas, shared or individual, and the means by which these are communicated.
Impact aesthetics (King)	The aggressive stylisation of editing and/or camera movement to physically shake the viewer.
Intensified continuity (Bordwell)	A commonly used modern style of continuity editing that uses tighter and shorter shots compared to earlier uses of continuity editing.
Intertextuality	The shaping of one text by other texts – the interrelationship between texts.
Iris	A circular frame on the shot, often isolating an important detail. Irises were commonly used in silent cinema for emphasis. A closing iris can also be used as a transition from one shot to another.
Jump cut	1. A shot that is arrhythmic or disjunctive and produces a noticeable skip between two shots, either because action isn't matched or shots break the 30° rule. 2. A cut that interrupts a single shot, literally producing a jump and an ellipsis in the action.
Key light	The brightest of three lights used in three-point lighting, this highlights details on the face by casting shadow on the unlit portion.
Kristeva, Julia	A French theorist of intertextuality, amongst other things.
Kuleshov effect	Named after Soviet film-maker Lev Kuleshov, an editing effect that creates an emotional effect by placing unrelated shots side by side.
Long shot (LS)	A shot in which human figures are just distinct, but background is still very visible.
Long take	A shot of long duration. One of cinema's most impressive techniques.
Low-angle shot	The camera is positioned below the subject, looking up. Low angles can often suggest a powerful subject who looms over us.
Low-key lighting	Lighting technique that creates dark pockets with little light on-screen (common in horror films).

Master (or establishing) shot	Often the first shot of a scene, the master, usually a long shot, shows us the whole scene, the setting, spatial relationships between characters and important action. Sometimes, whole scenes are shot in masters.
Match-on-action	Editing technique that matches line and movement of action from one shot to another.
Medium close-up (MCU)	A shot which shows individuals framed from the waist upwards; one of the most typical shots in television.
Medium long shot (MLS)	The human figure framed from around the knees upwards.
Metric montage (Eisenstein)	A montage effect in which the length of shots is determined arbitrarily and independently of the content of the images, by music or such.
Mise en scène	A critical term used of the organisation of objects within the camera's frame.
Montage	A general term for editing. Often associated with a montage sequence that condenses a lot of narrative information into a short space of time, or one that uses editing for a particular effect. Also a term for the kind of dialectical editing developed by Sergei Eisenstein.
Motif	A dominant idea or concept, a recurring formal element, colour or design feature. Repeated use of a particular shot distance can be developed into a motif through repetition and variation.
Narratology	A branch of Structuralism that examines narrative structure and narrative communication.
Noddy	Another name for a cutaway.
Non-diegetic	Anything in the film but not in its fictional world is referred to as non-diegetic (the score, credits, etc.).
Non-diegetic (or commentary) sound	Sound that does not emanate from objects or characters within the narrative fictional space, for example voice-over narration, soundtrack and so on.
Objective camera	Shots that allow the viewer a God-like perspective of the action without intruding on it.
Off-screen space	Space unseen by the camera, but implied by characters'/objects' movements, in dialogue or by sound.
On-screen space	The space seen by the camera.
Overcranking	The camera is run at more than 24 fps to produce smooth slow motion, sometimes up to around 2000 fps.
Overtonal montage (Eisenstein)	A montage effect that creates resonances in the conflict between dominant metric, rhythmic and tonal montage techniques used within a sequence.
Pan (panorama) shot	The camera turns left and right, as though turning its head on a horizontal plane.
Parallel editing	See cross-cutting.
Plan Américain ('American shot')	A French critical term for the medium long shot frequently used by Hollywood in the 1930s and 1940s.
Plot (Bordwell/Thompson)	The sum of story and non-diegetic elements, such as camera angles, editing, sound, titles, etc.
Point of view (POV) shot	Shots taken from the subjective perspective of a character or object in the film.
Profilmic event	The action filmed in front of the camera on location or in a studio before it is encoded into film language.
Propaganda	The tools used to deliberately influence the population.
Propp, Vladimir (1895–1970)	Russian critic and literary theorist.
Proscenium	A theatre stage or space that has a frame or arch as its main feature. Cinema still has very close links with theatre, and the camera frame was initially conceived as like a proscenium arch, as a window on the world.
Realism	A style of film-making that attempts to mimic material reality as closely as possible.
Reverse zoom	A special technique achieved by tracking toward a character while simultaneously zooming out, changing focal length and making the background stretch into the distance.
Rhythmic montage (Eisenstein)	A montage effect in which the length of shots is determined by the content of the images.

Semiotics The study of signs. It has its origins in the work of Ferdinand de Saussure, a Swiss linguist who was the first to identify some of the basic principles that apply to any sign-based system.

Sequence shot (Bazin) A sequence filmed in a single take in extreme depth of field.

Shot distance The distance of the shot in relation to the actor or object being filmed.

Shot-reverse-shot editing Pattern of shooting and editing often used for conversations, which cuts back and forth between shots following 180° and 30° rules with corresponding eyeline matches.

Sign Something which 'stands for' something else.

Sound perspective The apparent direction of sound reverberating in space. Perspective can be suggested by manipulating volume, echo and the balance in relation to other sounds in the diegesis.

Sound quality (Bordwell/Thompson) The properties exhibited by on-screen and off-screen sound; includes acoustic properties, such as loudness, pitch and timbre, and dimensions, including rhythm, fidelity, space and time.

Steadicam The camera is strapped to the camera operator using a special mount, which produces smooth, floating shots that are more flexible than tracking shots.

Story (Bordwell/Thompson) The linear construction of both represented and inferred narrative events.

Straight-on shot The camera pointed straight at its subject.

Structuralism A term applied to a body of thought that examines patterns of communication and meaning.

Subjective camera Shots that show us the world from the perspective of a character or object in the film.

Surrealism An artistic movement that explores subjective states of mind in dream states and was concerned with fragmentation.

Synchronous sound That which is heard at the same time that it is produced in the diegesis, for example dialogue or gun shots. Synchronised sound can be on-screen or off and is in time with the image.

Synecdoche Where some portion of a thing stands for the whole.

Text A verbal, written or visual artefact.

Three-point lighting The most common lighting technique, which uses three lights to ensure good exposure and give the illusion of a three-dimensional image.

Tilting shot The camera tilts up and down on a vertical line.

Tonal montage (Eisenstein) A montage effect that creates associations between the dominant emotional content of each shot.

Tracking (dolly or trucking) shot The camera moves on a fixed track, which can be laid in any direction.

Undercranking The camera is run at slower than 24 frames per second (fps) to produce faster motion on playback.

Urtext An original or the earliest version of a text, to which later versions can be compared.

Wipe A transition in which a line wipes one shot from the screen, which is replaced by the next.

Zoom A lens fitted to the camera that allows the operator to change the focal length and alter the dimension of the image; produces moving shots without requiring the camera to move physically.

Recommended reading

Chapter 1:
Semiotics

Introductory reading

- Braudy, Leo & Marshall Cohen (eds). *Film Theory and Criticism: Introductory Readings*, 7th Ed. New York and Oxford: Oxford University Press 2009
- Hayward, Susan. *Key Concepts in Cinema Studies*. London: Routledge 2006
- Monaco, James. *How to Read a Film*. New York and Oxford: Oxford University Press 2000

Advanced reading

- Barthes, Roland. *S/Z: An Essay*. New York: Hill and Wang 1972
- Buckland, Warren. *The Cognitive Semiotics of Film*. Cambridge University Press 2007
- Metz, Christian. *Film Language: A Semiotics of the Cinema*. Chicago: University of Chicago Press 1990
- Mitry, Jean. *Semiotics and the Analysis of Film*. Indiana University Press 2000
- Wollen, Peter. *Signs and Meanings in the Cinema*, 4th Ed. London: BFI 1998

Chapter 2:
Narrative

Introductory reading

- Bordwell, David & Kristin Thompson. *Film Art: An Introduction*, 8th Ed. London: McGraw-Hill 2008
- Lothe, Jakob. *Narrative in Fiction and Film*. New York: Oxford University Press 2000
- Monaco, James. *How to Read a Film*. New York and Oxford: Oxford University Press 2000
- Stam, Burgoyne and Flitterman-Lewis. *New Vocabularies in Film Semiotics*. London: Routledge 1992

Advanced reading

- Chatman, Seymour. *Story and Structure: Narrative Structure in Fiction and Film*. Cornell University Press 1980
- Fabe, Marilyn. *Closely Watched Films: An Introduction to the Art of Narrative Film Techniques*. California: University of California Press 2004
- Genette, Gérard. *Narrative Discourse: An Essay in Method*, Cornell University Press 1983

Chapter 3:
Intertextuality

Introductory reading

- Hayward, Susan. *Key Concepts in Cinema Studies*. London: Routledge 2006
- Orr, Mary. *Intertextuality: Debates and Contexts*. Polity 2003
- Stam, Burgoyne and Flitterman-Lewis. *New Vocabularies in Film Semiotics*. London: Routledge 1992

Advanced reading

- Bauman, Richard. *A World of Other's Words: Cross Cultural Perspectives on Intertextuality*. London: Blackwell 2004
- Boyd and Palmer. *After Hitchcock: Influence, Imitation and Intertextuality*. Austin: University of Texas Press 2006
- Kristeva, Julia. *The Kristeva Reader*. New York: Columbia University Press 1986
- Sanders, Julie. *Adaptation and Appropriation*. London: Routledge 2005

Chapter 4:
Ideology

Introductory reading

- Braudy, Leo & Marshall Cohen (eds). *Film Theory and Criticism: Introductory Readings*, 7th Ed. New York and Oxford: Oxford University Press 2009
- Dix, Andrew. *Beginning Film Studies*. Manchester: Manchester University Press 2008

Advanced reading

- Bazin, André. *What is Cinema?* 2 Vols. Berkeley, California; London: University of California Press, 1967–1972
- Bordwell, David. *Figures Traced in Light: On Cinematic Staging*. Berkeley; London. University of California Press, 2005
- Eagleton, Terry. *Ideology: An Introduction*. London: Verso 2006
- Kracauer, Seigfried. *Theory of Film: The Redemption of Physical Reality*. Princeton, N. J. : Princeton University Press 1997
- Lapsley and Westlake. *Film Theory: An Introduction*, 2nd Ed. Manchester: Manchester University Press 2006.

Chapter 5:
Frames and images

Introductory reading

- Dix, Andrew. *Beginning Film Studies*. Manchester: Manchester University Press 2008

Advanced reading

- Bazin, André. *What is Cinema?* 2 Vols. Berkeley, California; London: University of California Press, 1967–1972
- Bordwell, David. *Figures Traced in Light: On Cinematic Staging*. Berkeley; London. University of California Press, 2005.
- François, Truffaut. *Hitchcock*. New York; London: Simon and Schuster, 1985
- King, Geoff. *Spectacular Narratives: Hollywood in the Age of the Blockbuster*. London: I. B. Tauris 2000
- Kracauer, Seigfried. *Theory of Film: The Redemption of Physical Reality*. Princeton, N. J. : Princeton University Press 1997
- Wollen, Peter. *Signs and Meanings in the Cinema*, 4th Ed. London: BFI 1998

Chapter 6:
Constructing meaning

Introductory reading

- Altman, Rick. *Sound Theory Sound Practice*. London: Routledge 1992
- Dancyger, Ken. *The Technique of Film and Video Editing: History, Theory and Practice*. Oxford: Focal 2007
- Orpen, Valerie. *Film Editing: The Art of the Expressive*. London: Wallflower 2003
- Sider, Larry. *Soundscape: The School of Sound Lectures, 1998–2001*. London: Wallflower 2003

Advanced reading

- Chion, Michel. *Audio-Vision: Sound on Screen*. New York: Columbia University Press 1994
- Eisenstein, Sergei. *Film Form: Essays in Film Theory*. New York: Harcourt 1969
- Murch, Walter. *In the Blink of an Eye: A Perspective on Film Editing*. Los Angeles, California : Silman-James 2001
- Sonnenschein, David. *Sound Design: The Expressive Power of Music, Voice, and Sound Effects in Cinema* Sound City: Michael Wiese Productions 2001

Cover image:
The Wizard of Oz (1939)
courtesy of MGM / The Kobal Collection.

Page 2:
Pan's Labyrinth (2006)
courtesy of Tequila Gang/WB /
The Kobal Collection.

Page 9:
The Boy in the Striped Pajamas (2008)
courtesy of Heyday Films /
The Kobal Collection.

Page 12:
Grease (1978)
courtesy of Paramount /
The Kobal Collection.

Page 15:
Bride throwing bouquet © iofoto.
Courtesy of Shutterstock.com.

Page 17:
Peeping Tom (1960)
courtesy of Anglo Amalgamated /
The Kobal Collection.

Page 18:
Dead Sheriff © Drazen Vukelic.
Courtesy of Shutterstock.com.

Page 24:
Red rose © tkachuk.
Courtesy of Shutterstock.com.

Pages 54 and 176:
Retro movies background © Maugli.
Courtesy of Shutterstock.com.

Page 20:
The Pillow Book (1995)
courtesy of Kasander & Wigman/
Alpha Films / The Kobal Collection /
Mark Guillamot.

Page 27:
The Birth of a Nation (1915)
courtesy of Epoch /
The Kobal Collection.

Page 31:
Falling Down (1993)
courtesy of Warner Bros /
The Kobal Collection.

Page 32:
Seven (1995)
courtesy of New Line /
The Kobal Collection / Peter Sorel.

Page 37:
Seven (1995)
courtesy of New Line / The Kobal Collection.

Page 38:
Zardoz (1973)
courtesy of 20th Century Fox /
The Kobal Collection.

Page 40:
Handshape © xjbxjhxm123.
Courtesy of Shutterstock.com.

Page 46:
Memento (2000)
courtesy of Summit Entertainment /
The Kobal Collection /
Danny Rothenberg.

Page 56:
Forrest Gump (1994)
courtesy of Paramount /
The Kobal Collection.

Page 59:
Manhunter (1986)
courtesy of De Laurentiis Group /
The Kobal Collection.

Pages 60–67 and 153:
Cheap Beans (2008)
courtesy of Lithium Heart Productions /
York St John University.

Page 68:
Frankenstein (1994)
courtesy of Tri-Star/American Zoetrope /
The Kobal Collection.

Page 71:
Embroidery © Vasina Natalia.
Courtesy of Shutterstock.com.

Page 72:
Die Hard (1988)
courtesy of 20th Century Fox /
The Kobal Collection / Peter Sorel.

Page 75:
Play it again, Sam (1972)
courtesy of Paramount /
The Kobal Collection.

Page 77:
Scream 2 (1997)
courtesy of Dimension Films /
The Kobal Collection.

Page 81:
The Matrix (1999)
courtesy of Warner Bros /
The Kobal Collection / Jasin Boland.

Page 84:
Twisted celluloid © Granite.
Courtesy of Shutterstock.com.

Page 90:
Citizen Kane (1941)
courtesy of RKO / The Kobal Collection.

Page 93:
Citizen Kane (1941)
courtesy of RKO /
The Kobal Collection / Alex Kahle.

Page 94:
How I won the war (1967)
courtesy of United Artists /
The Kobal Collection.

Page 101:
Dirty Harry (1971)
courtesy of Warner Bros /
The Kobal Collection.

Page 106:
The Hill (1965)
courtesy of MGM/7 Arts /
The Kobal Collection.

Page 108:
Feston (1998)
courtesy of Nimbus Film /
The Kobal Collection.

Pages 112–116, 128 and 155:
Without Wires (2008)
courtesy of Batmen Productions/Sun
Entertainment / York St John University.

Page 118:
The Good, the Bad and the Ugly (1966)
courtesy of P.E.A / The Kobal Collection.

Page 120:
High-tech eye background © lavitrei.
Courtesy of Shutterstock.com.

Page 126:
Singin' in the Rain (1952)
courtesy of MGM / The Kobal Collection.

Page 130:
Don't Look Now (1973)
courtesy of Casey Prods-Eldorado Films /
The Kobal Collection.

Page 133:
Eternal Sunshine of the Spotless Mind
(2004) courtesy of Focus Features /
The Kobal Collection / David Lee.

Page 134:
Camera close-up © Caroline.
Courtesy of Shutterstock.com.

Page 139:
In the Mood for Love (2000)
courtesy of Block 2 Pics / Jet Tone /
The Kobal Collection.

Pages 140–147:
Without Tyres (2008) courtesy
of Elephant Productions.

Page 148:
CQ (2001)
courtesy of Zoetrope / Ua /
The Kobal Collection / Jean-Paul Kieffer.

Page 152:
Reel cases © Carsten Reisinger.
Courtesy Shutterstock.com.

Page 160:
Un Chien Andalou (1929)
courtesy of Bunuel-Dali /
The Kobal Collection.

Page 162:
Young woman © Creatista.
Cheese and wine © Karin Lan.
Courtesy of Shutterstock.com.

Page 163:
Rear Window (1954)
courtesy of Paramount /
The Kobal Collection.

Page 165:
Battleship Potemkin (1925)
courtesy of Goskino /
The Kobal Collection.

Page 169:
McCabe and Mrs Miller (1971)
courtesy of Warner Bros /
The Kobal Collection.

Page 176:
Film strip © djem.
Courtesy of Shutterstock.com.

Publisher's note

The subject of ethics is not new, yet its consideration within the applied visual arts is perhaps not as prevalent as it might be. Our aim here is to help a new generation of students, educators and practitioners find a methodology for structuring their thoughts and reflections in this vital area.

AVA Publishing hopes that these **Working with ethics** pages provide a platform for consideration and a flexible method for incorporating ethical concerns in the work of educators, students and professionals. Our approach consists of four parts:

The **introduction** is intended to be an accessible snapshot of the ethical landscape, both in terms of historical development and current dominant themes.

The **framework** positions ethical consideration into four areas and poses questions about the practical implications that might occur. Marking your response to each of these questions on the scale shown will allow your reactions to be further explored by comparison.

The **case study** sets out a real project and then poses some ethical questions for further consideration. This is a focus point for a debate rather than a critical analysis so there are no predetermined right or wrong answers.

A selection of **further reading** for you to consider areas of particular interest in more detail.

Ethical: aware-
ness/
reflect-
ion/
debate

Working with ethics

Introduction

Ethics is a complex subject that interlaces the idea of responsibilities to society with a wide range of considerations relevant to the character and happiness of the individual. It concerns virtues of compassion, loyalty and strength, but also of confidence, imagination, humour and optimism. As introduced in ancient Greek philosophy, the fundamental ethical question is: *what should I do?* How we might pursue a 'good' life not only raises moral concerns about the effects of our actions on others, but also personal concerns about our own integrity.

In modern times the most important and controversial questions in ethics have been the moral ones. With growing populations and improvements in mobility and communications, it is not surprising that considerations about how to structure our lives together on the planet should come to the forefront. For visual artists and communicators, it should be no surprise that these considerations will enter into the creative process.

Some ethical considerations are already enshrined in government laws and regulations or in professional codes of conduct. For example, plagiarism and breaches of confidentiality can be punishable offences. Legislation in various nations makes it unlawful to exclude people with disabilities from accessing information or spaces. The trade of ivory as a material has been banned in many countries. In these cases, a clear line has been drawn under what is unacceptable.

But most ethical matters remain open to debate, among experts and lay-people alike, and in the end we have to make our own choices on the basis of our own guiding principles or values. Is it more ethical to work for a charity than for a commercial company? Is it unethical to create something that others find ugly or offensive?

Specific questions such as these may lead to other questions that are more abstract. For example, is it only effects on humans (and what they care about) that are important, or might effects on the natural world require attention too?

Is promoting ethical consequences justified even when it requires ethical sacrifices along the way? Must there be a single unifying theory of ethics (such as the Utilitarian thesis that the right course of action is always the one that leads to the greatest happiness of the greatest number), or might there always be many different ethical values that pull a person in various directions?

As we enter into ethical debate and engage with these dilemmas on a personal and professional level, we may change our views or change our view of others. The real test though is whether, as we reflect on these matters, we change the way we act as well as the way we think. Socrates, the 'father' of philosophy, proposed that people will naturally do 'good' if they know what is right. But this point might only lead us to yet another question: *how do we know what is right?*

Working with ethics

You
What are your ethical beliefs?

Central to everything you do will be your attitude to people and issues around you. For some people, their ethics are an active part of the decisions they make every day as a consumer, a voter or a working professional. Others may think about ethics very little and yet this does not automatically make them unethical. Personal beliefs, lifestyle, politics, nationality, religion, gender, class or education can all influence your ethical viewpoint.

Using the scale, where would you place yourself? What do you take into account to make your decision? Compare results with your friends or colleagues.

Your client
What are your terms?

Working relationships are central to whether ethics can be embedded into a project, and your conduct on a day-to-day basis is a demonstration of your professional ethics. The decision with the biggest impact is whom you choose to work with in the first place. Cigarette companies or arms traders are often-cited examples when talking about where a line might be drawn, but rarely are real situations so extreme. At what point might you turn down a project on ethical grounds and how much does the reality of having to earn a living affect your ability to choose?

Using the scale, where would you place a project? How does this compare to your personal ethical level?

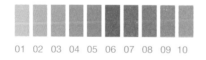

01 02 03 04 05 06 07 08 09 10

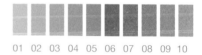

01 02 03 04 05 06 07 08 09 10

Your specifications
What are the impacts of your materials?

In relatively recent times, we are learning that many natural materials are in short supply. At the same time, we are increasingly aware that some man-made materials can have harmful, long-term effects on people or the planet. How much do you know about the materials that you use? Do you know where they come from, how far they travel and under what conditions they are obtained? When your creation is no longer needed, will it be easy and safe to recycle? Will it disappear without a trace? Are these considerations your responsibility or are they out of your hands?

Using the scale, mark how ethical your material choices are.

Your creation
What is the purpose of your work?

Between you, your colleagues and an agreed brief, what will your creation achieve? What purpose will it have in society and will it make a positive contribution? Should your work result in more than commercial success or industry awards? Might your creation help save lives, educate, protect or inspire? Form and function are two established aspects of judging a creation, but there is little consensus on the obligations of visual artists and communicators toward society, or the role they might have in solving social or environmental problems. If you want recognition for being the creator, how responsible are you for what you create and where might that responsibility end?

Using the scale, mark how ethical the purpose of your work is.

Working with ethics

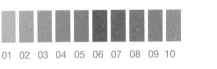

01 02 03 04 05 06 07 08 09 10

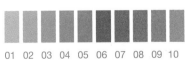

01 02 03 04 05 06 07 08 09 10

One aspect of film-making that raises an ethical dilemma is the use of historical subjects as storylines. Many filmgoers are known to obtain their understanding of historical events from films and many popular films are based, although sometimes loosely, on historical happenings. But when these films are created as stories rather than factual documentaries, how much responsibility does a film-maker have for portraying an accurate account? Should the film-maker have artistic license to use historical material selectively in order to entertain? Is a film-maker an interpreter rather than a reporter? If so, why is the opinion of the film-maker able to carry more influence than that of anyone else? Is the viewer expected to know the difference between a documentary film and a work of entertainment? When historians differ in their understanding or interpretation of what actually happened, does it matter if the historical details in a film are wrong or inaccurate? Should the intentions of the film-maker ultimately be the point of scrutiny, with the assumption being that the deliberate distortion of facts is more unethical than historical adaptations, if used solely for increased dramatic effect?

As a young man, Denis Kaufman witnessed the 1917 Russian Revolution. In this momentous historical event, the last Czar of Russia was replaced by the Russian Provisional Government, which was then itself removed and replaced by a Bolshevik (Communist) government. In 1918, Kaufman was hired as an assistant at the Moscow Cinema Committee and renamed himself Dziga Vertov (translated as 'spinning top' or 'spinning gypsy').

Vertov began to edit documentary footage on weekly Soviet newsreels. Earlier First World War newsreels typically used images as dry evidence of named places, for example, but were not combined to construct an argument. Vertov structured his films journalistically, using associations and links between elements; thereby creating a persuasive and analytical approach that he hoped would grab the viewers. Along with his wife and his brother, Vertov developed the concept of *kino-pravda* (translated as 'film-truth') through his newsreel series of the same name. His aim was to capture fragments of reality which, when organised together, might reveal a deeper, more fundamental truth.